Here's a list of the keystrokes you can use to quickly choose the most popular Excel commands. If you have a mouse and like to use it, everything here can also be accomplished by clicking on tools on the various toolbars.

Mini-Reference

Common Windows Tasks

If you want to...	Press...
Show the next worksheet that's open in Excel	Ctrl+F6
Close a worksheet that's on your screen	Ctrl+F4
Leave Excel for the moment, and go to another Windows program that's running on your computer	Alt+Tab
Quit Excel	Alt+F4

Common Worksheet Tasks

If you want to...	Press...
Open a new, blank worksheet	Shift+F11
Open a saved worksheet	Ctrl+F12
Save a worksheet	Shift+F12
Change the name of a saved worksheet	F12
Print a worksheet	Ctrl+Shift+F12

Common Movement Tasks

If you want to...	Press...
Move down to the next row	↓
Move up to the preceding row	↑
Move to cell A1 from anywhere in the worksheet	Ctrl+Home
Move to the beginning of a row	Home
Move down one window	PgDn
Move up one window	PgUp
Move to the end of a cell range that contains data	End+Arrow key
Move to the last cell that contains data in the worksheet	End+Home

Common Entering & Editing Tasks

If you want to...	Press...
Edit the contents of a cell in the formula	F2
Clear out the contents of a cell	Del
Copy a cell	Ctrl+C or Ctrl+Ins
Cut a cell	Ctrl+X or Shift+Del
Paste the cell you just cut or copied	Ctrl+V or Shift+Ins
Undo an operation	Ctrl+Z
Sum a range of cells	Alt+= when the first blank cell below the range you want to sum is the active cell

Common Formatting Tasks

If you want to...	Do this...
Make cells bold	Select the target cells and press Ctrl+B
Make cells italic	Select the target cells and press Ctrl+I
Choose a different font name	Select the target cells, press Ctrl+F, type the name of the font, and press Enter
Choose a different point size	Select the target cells, press Ctrl+P, type the point size, and press Enter

Common Function Keys: The Best of the Rest

If you want to...	Press...
Display a help window	F1
Activate the menu bar so that you can open a menu	F10 or Alt
Show the shortcut menu for a cell	Shift+F10
Recalculate your worksheet formulas	F9
Go to any cell in the worksheet	F5
Move to the next pane of a split window	F6
Paste a function in the formula bar	Shift+F3

I HATE
EXCEL

Patrick J. Burns

I Hate Excel

Copyright © 1993 by Que® Corporation

All rights reserved. Printed in the United States of America. No part of this book may be used or reproduced in any form or by any means, or stored in a database or retrieval system, without prior written permission of the publisher except in the case of brief quotations embodied in critical articles and reviews. Making copies of any part of this book for any purpose other than your own personal use is a violation of United States copyright laws. For information, address Que Corporation, 11711 N. College Ave., Carmel, IN 46032.

Library of Congress Catalog No.: 93-83389

ISBN: 1-56529-213-8

This book is sold *as is*, without warranty of any kind, either express or implied, respecting the contents of this book, including but not limited to implied warranties for the book's quality, performance, merchantability, or fitness for any particular purpose. Neither Que Corporation nor its dealers or distributors shall be liable to the purchaser or any other person or entity with respect to any liability, loss, or damage caused or alleged to have been caused directly or indirectly by this book.

95 94 93   6 5 4 3 2 1

Interpretation of the printing code: the rightmost double-digit number is the year of the book's printing; the rightmost single-digit number, the number of the book's printing. For example, a printing code of 93-1 shows that the first printing of the book occurred in 1993.

Screen reproductions in this book were created using Collage Plus from Inner Media, Inc., Hollis, NH.

I Hate Excel is based on Microsoft Excel Version 4.0.

Publisher: Lloyd J. Short

Associate Publisher: Rick Ranucci

Publishing Plan Manager: Thomas H. Bennett

Operations Manager: Sheila Cunningham

Acquisitions Editor: Chris Katsaropoulos

Dedication

Three people in my life, each a stranger to the other, have been kind enough to share their wit and wisdom. Jack Burns, who convinced me to plant my feet firmly in the ground before allowing my mind to drift off to the stars. Kenny Baca, who taught me to stop and smell the roses before I bundled them up and shipped them out. Patty Vergara, the first person I ever met who hated computers more than I did. My eternal soul mate. One day I'd like to get you all together in one place and say, "Now look what you've gone and done!"

About the Author

Patrick J. Burns is a well-entrenched author, a self-professed spreadsheet guru, and a really happy guy. A founder and principal of Burns & Associates, a professional consulting firm, Patrick has authored lots of 400-pound computer books. It's the experience he's garnered from his other professions—wrapping fruit, cutting grass at a golf course, and selling flowers—that has allowed him to become so conversant in matters of silicon chips and plastic mice. He welcomes all comments and criticisms about the book. Send them in care of Waterside Productions, 2191 San Elijo Avenue, Cardiff-by-the-Sea, California 92007.

When Patrick gets bored with writing, he hops on a plane and darts off to exotic locations around the world. Always one to adapt to local culture, he's played cards with banditos in a Mexican jail, trekked the Himalayas on camel, and explored a sunken Greek freighter 110 feet below the ocean surface off the coast of Barbados. One time he ended up in a gigantic black stew pot deep in the jungle of a South Pacific island. Patrick loves to play beach volleyball, hates snails and gigantic black stew pots, is 6'1" tall, has brown hair and eyes, sometimes dreams in French, and adores his blond-haired and blue-eyed, 5' 9" girlfriend, Cathy.

I HATE EXCEL!

Credits

Title Manager:
Shelley O'Hara

Production Editor:
Barbara K. Koenig

Editor:
Heather Northrup

Technical Editor:
Anne Poirson

Book Designer:
Scott Cook

Illustrations:
Jeff MacNelly

Novice Reviewer:
Kathy Roche

Editorial Assistants:
Julia Blount
Sandra Naito

Production Team:
Julie Brown
Jodie Cantwell
Laurie Casey
Brook Farling
Jay Lesandrini
Heather Kaufman
Caroline Roop
Linda Seifert
Susan VandeWalle
Mary Beth Wakefield

Indexers:
Caroline Roop
Tina Trettin

Composed in *Goudy* and *MCPdigital* by Que Corporation.

Acknowledgments

Where do I begin? It's like being shipwrecked on a deserted island with 30 strangers who suddenly become your closest friends. Half the time is spent imagining so-and-so smothered in a creamy béarnaise sauce, while the rest is spent exchanging ideas, solving problems, or just talking dirty. Then suddenly you're rescued, and it's time to bid everyone farewell.

At Que: Many thanks to Shelley O'Hara, my alter ego on this book. Had I known earlier that not hearing from you meant that all was going well, I would have turned off the phones sooner. Thanks to Rick, Don, and Chris, for excellent coaching. And thanks to Barbara Koenig, for your friendly voice, easy-to-answer questions, and your careful attention to detail.

At home: Thanks, Cathy, for being such a good sport throughout this shipwreck. You listened to me, read for me, advised me, coaxed me, consoled me, cajoled me, and celebrated with me without complaining (too much) or quitting (ever). You deserve 100 medals!

At Waterside: Thanks, Bill and Matt, for the vote of confidence on this one. Carol, thanks for managing the money. Lavander, Margo, and Kristin, thanks for understanding when I get your voices mixed up on the phone.

Trademark Acknowledgments

All terms mentioned in this book that are known to be trademarks or service marks have been appropriately capitalized. Que cannot attest to the accuracy of this information. Use of a term in this book should not be regarded as affecting the validity of any trademark or service mark.

Microsoft Excel and Microsoft Windows are registered trademarks of Microsoft Corporation.

Contents at a Glance

Contents

I HATE EXCEL!

I HATE EXCEL!

Introduction

"Hey, what happened to my mouse pointer?"

"My data disappeared!!"

"I hate Excel!"

"#$?/%@!"

Famous first and last words. They roll off every computer user's tongue at one time or another. Hey, computers are tricky. Excel can be tricky. But it really isn't too difficult to outsmart both of them. All you need is this book. This is a book about Excel for people who hate the thought of learning Excel. Of learning anything. This is a book for people who just want to get things done.

Throughout this book I do my best to talk *to* you—not *at* you. If ever you feel that I've let you down in this regard, tear out the offending pages and mail them back to me. I'll promptly rewrite them and send them back. You see, when confronted with six different ways of doing the same thing in Excel, I choose to ignore at least five of them. We'll learn only the stuff that gets you immediate results, like a great-looking budget report, a well-organized printout, and a hefty raise. Well, I can't promise that last one.

Icons

(What those little pictures really mean)

I promised you that I'd only discuss the things that are relevant to the basics of using Excel. By and large, this goal has been accomplished. But every so often, it gets tough to complete a thought without mentioning some technical buzzword, esoteric computer function, or obscure mathematical concept. That's why you'll see a bunch of little picture icons.

The pictures that appear in the margins of this book are dedicated to completing thoughts, filling in blanks, stopping you from self-destructing, and ushering you into nerddom. Actually, feel free to skip over all the stuff flagged with icons, because it won't impair your ability to successfully work in Excel. But if you're feeling a little bit adventurous some morning, take a look at the information in those parts.

Here are the pictures and what they mean:

TIP

This icon alerts you to shortcuts, tricks, and time-savers.

EXPERTS ONLY

This icon flags the really technical stuff. If you are curious, read this information. And remember, curiosity killed the cat, but satisfaction brought him back.

"I HATE THIS!"

This icon points out all the frustrating, annoying problems you might encounter.

CAUTION

This icon says: "Hey! Watch Out! Stop! Falling Rocks Ahead!"

BUZZWORDS

This icon warns you that you're about to learn an impressive technicobabble word.

PART I

All You Really Need To Know

Includes:

CHAPTER 1

Getting Started
(The Secrets of a Spreadsheet, Uncovered)

IN A NUTSHELL

▼ What's a spreadsheet?

▼ What's Excel?

▼ Starting Excel

▼ Checking out the territory

▼ Moving around in a worksheet

▼ Typing stuff (or stuffing type) into a worksheet

The original inspiration for a spreadsheet arose from a pretty basic need: the need to count things. It didn't matter what you were counting—beans, sheep, rocks, money. You just needed a way to know how many beans, or whatever, you had. The counting started on fingers, moved to those bead things called abacuses, and then took a leap onto paper.

The original spreadsheets were big pieces of ruled paper you could spread out on a table top. You'd scribble numbers on each sheet, being very careful to stay between the lines, and then total them up with a calculator. Then along came computers, and spreadsheets became high-tech and electronic.

Today's spreadsheets can do lots more than count stones and rice grains. This chapter introduces to you the modern-day spreadsheet.

BUZZWORDS

SPREADSHEET

A spreadsheet is a program designed to let you tinker around with numbers. It's the high-tech equivalent of a ledger sheet and calculator.

The Secret of a Spreadsheet

The best way to get a feel for a spreadsheet program like Excel is to start with something familiar, like a personal budget. The following worksheet shows a short list of expenses that should look familiar to you. The number at the bottom of these expenses is their total.

The Monthly Bills Budget
for June, 1993

A typical
personal
budget

	Budgeted	Actual	Over/ Under (-)
Mortgage payment	$1,250.25	$1,250.25	$0.00
Vacation fund	100.00	100.00	0.00
College fund	200.00	0.00	-200.00
Fun stuff	200.00	600.00	400.00
Food	225.00	234.21	9.21
Car payment	225.57	225.57	0.00
Gas & electric	37.00	62.87	25.87
Cable	40.00	41.54	1.54
Telephone	68.00	59.66	-8.34
Car gas & upkeep	75.00	89.93	14.93
Totals:	$2,420.82	$2,664.03	$243.21

You can easily total the numbers with a calculator, but what if something changes? What if you want to add something? What if you are a multimillionaire and your budget includes lots of categories such as furs, diamonds, Jaguars, and so on? For any of these scenarios, you'd have to peck, peck, peck through the numbers all over again on the calculator.

With Excel, you just change, add, or delete a number, and the totals are recalculated automatically. And that, my friends, is the beauty of a spreadsheet program!

Giving Excel the Green Light

To put that magic to work, you first have to start Excel. That involves figuring out where you are starting from. If you turn on the computer and see Excel already, you are lucky! Skip this entire section. If you see something like C:\>, you have to start Windows first. Read the next two sections. If you see Windows, go directly to the section called "I See Windows." Do not pass Go.

I See C:\> or Some Variation

If you see pretty much a blank screen with C:\> or something like that, you are at the DOS prompt. You first have to start Windows. Type **win** and press Enter. You should see a bunch of little pictures on-screen. That's the Program Manager, alias Windows. (If you want to learn all the ins and outs of Windows, get a copy of *I Hate Windows*. I've got enough to worry about teaching you Excel.)

I See Windows

OK. Somehow or other you see Windows. Either you started it yourself or you turned on your computer and it magically appeared (someone— the person who sold you the computer, your sister-in-law the computer whiz, or your son—has set up the computer so that this happens automatically). Now you are ready to start Excel.

Look around on your screen for an icon (a little picture) that says *Microsoft Excel 4.0* or something like that.

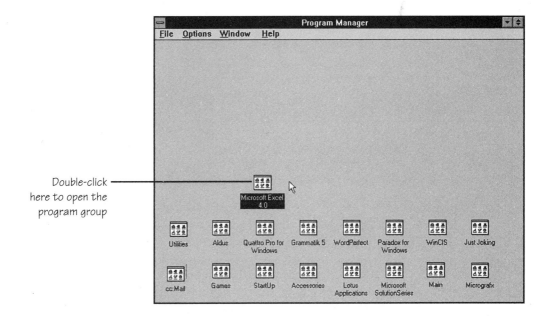

Double-click
here to open the
program group

Now grab hold of your mouse and slide it on your desk until the arrow
on your screen is positioned directly on the icon. Press the left mouse
button twice, really quickly. This is called *double-clicking*. A window will
open and inside you should see an icon called *Microsoft Excel*. Point to
this icon and double-click the mouse button. Excel starts!

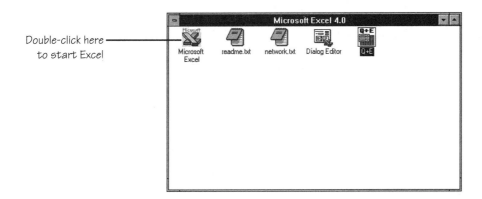

Double-click here
to start Excel

TIP

In Excel you can use a mouse to do things like move around on-screen, click icons to start activities, and scroll the worksheet on your screen. All this—and more—is possible when you acquaint yourself with the three dance steps necessary to tango with your mouse:

Click	Press and release the mouse button in one continuous motion.
Double-click	Press and release the mouse button, then do it again, really quickly.
Drag	Press and hold down the mouse button and drag the mouse pointer around on your screen; when you're finished dragging, release the button.

Looking Under the Hood

(What makes this thing go?)

The Excel worksheet is really nothing more than a grid of columns and rows. It's the electronic version of an accountant's ledger sheet, but the columns and rows are identified.

BUZZWORDS

WORKSHEET

A worksheet is the grid of columns and rows. It's where you type your numbers. In Excel, you see each worksheet in its own window.

A column in a worksheet is identified by a letter. The first column is column A, the second is column B, and so on. Each row is identified by a number: 1, 2, 3, 4, and so on. Take a look at this worksheet:

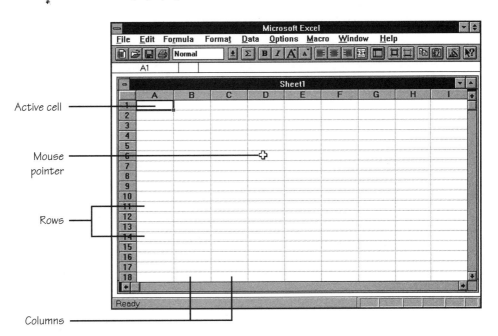

Active cell

Mouse pointer

Rows

Columns

Now take a look at where column A meets row 1 in the worksheet. This is called a *cell*. The "address" of the cell is formed by snapping together the column letter and row number, such as A1. Notice that cell A1 has a dark rectangle around it. The cell with the dark rectangle is called the *active cell*.

BUZZWORDS

CELL ADDRESS

A cell address is the name of the cell and is formed by combining the column letter and row number.

BUZZWORDS

ACTIVE CELL

The active cell is where Excel will store words and numbers when you type them from your keyboard.

You probably see only 9 or so columns and 16 or so rows, but this is really only the top left corner of a much larger beast. Excel has 256 columns and 16,384 rows! You'll only see a few rows and columns on-screen at any one time because your screen isn't large enough to show everything.

TIP

If you bump the keyboard and the active cell suddenly changes location and you can no longer see your original worksheet area, hold down the Ctrl key and press the Home key. Pressing Ctrl plus Home yanks the active cell back to A1. Sort of like bungee jumping into and out of the Grand Canyon.

Checking Out the Dashboard

(What's all this stuff on my screen?)

The area just above the worksheet on your screen is Excel's equivalent of an automobile dashboard. The gadgets you see are the controls you use to "drive" Excel.

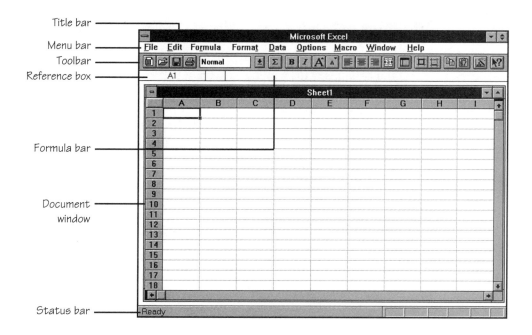

Title bar

Menu bar

Toolbar

Reference box

Formula bar

Document window

Status bar

Excel's dashboard

▼ The top title bar displays the name of the program, Microsoft Excel.

▼ The menu bar lists the menus: File, Edit, Help, and so on.

▼ The toolbar contains lots of little icons you can use to do stuff quickly in Excel. More about that later.

▼ The reference box displays the address of the active cell.

▼ The formula bar is where Excel displays what you type, before you stick it in the active cell.

▼ The Irish Bar (not shown here) is on Carmel Mountain Road in San Diego, California. Ask for John. Tell him Pat sent you.

continues

I HATE EXCEL!

Excel's dashboard, continued

▼ The document window contains the worksheet—the grid of rows and columns. This window also has a title bar, and it probably says SHEET1.

▼ The status bar displays plain-English descriptions of many activities that take place while you're driving around in Excel.

TIP

When you can't figure out what's happening in Excel, check the status bar first. The message you see there might call attention to a problem or condition that isn't readily evident to the untrained eye.

Moving Around

(Finger-twisting fun)

Before you can begin typing away, you first have to pick the active cell—the cell you want to put something in. There are a bunch of different ways to move the active cell around the worksheet.

To move the active cell with your mouse, move the mouse pointer (the four-pointed cross that looks like a plus symbol) around the worksheet on your screen until it rests on the cell you want to make active. Then click the left mouse button.

To move the active cell with your keyboard, just press one of the four keys marked with an arrow. The active cell moves in the direction of the arrow, one cell at a time.

Other keys you can use to cruise

▼ To make cell A1 the active cell, hold down the Ctrl key and press the Home key.

▼ To quickly move more than one cell in any direction, press the End key and then press the arrow key that points in the direction you're heading. If you get numbers instead of moving, your Num Lock key is on. Press the Num Lock key again to turn it off.

▼ Press the PgUp and PgDn keys to scroll the worksheet up and down, one screen at a time.

▼ To go to a specific cell, press the F5 function key, type the cell's address, and press Enter.

How To Enter Information

Entering information into a new worksheet is as easy as selecting the lucky cell, doing a little typing, and then pressing Enter.

Golden rules for entering stuff into worksheet cells

▼ Whenever you begin typing anything on your keyboard, the characters will appear in the formula bar. You can watch as you type. If you make a mistake, press Backspace to delete the error, and then retype the information.

▼ To store stuff in the active cell after you finish typing it, just press Enter.

continues

Golden rules for entering stuff into worksheet cells, continued

▼ If you change your mind before pressing Enter, press Esc. Nothing is entered in the cell. If you've already pressed Enter, read the next chapter to find out how to correct your mistake.

▼ To store stuff in the active cell and then advance to a cell in a particular direction, just press the up-, down-, left-, or right-arrow key instead of pressing Enter.

▼ As you type, you'll see two boxes to the left of the text: one contains an X and the other shows a check mark. You can click on the check mark, rather than pressing Enter, to enter the information into the cell. Click on the X box to cancel the entry.

What You Can Enter

You know how to enter stuff; now you need to figure out what to enter. Basically, you can enter words, numbers, dates, or formulas.

"I HATE THIS!"

Is it a number? Is it text?

Excel handles different types of information differently. For instance, Excel can subtract two dates or two numbers, but it can't subtract text. It's important that you and Excel "agree" on the type of information you are entering. If you think you are entering a number, Excel better think it's a number, too. If you think you've entered a date, Excel better think it's a date. Most of the time, you don't have to worry about this, because Excel and you will be in agreement.

Putting It into Words

To type text into a cell, select the cell and type the text you want. For instance, click on cell B1, type **My Finances**, and press Enter. Excel enters the text into the selected cell.

Checklist

▼ As long as the entry contains at least one letter, or a character such as * ! & # or ?, Excel will treat your entry as text. (That is, unless Excel thinks it's a negative number, scientific notation, date, time, or formula. Read the rest of the chapter for the gory details on this.)

▼ You can type other characters (ones that aren't letters of the alphabet) as part of the entry. This includes things like numbers and punctuation characters.

▼ Excel automatically aligns text to the left edge of the cell.

▼ When the entry is so long that it won't fit into the width of the current cell, Excel allows the extra characters to spill over into the cell immediately to the right, as long as that cell is empty. (The extra characters aren't actually *in* the adjacent cell; they're just displayed there.) If that cell does contain information, you won't see your entire cell entry, because part of it won't be displayed. But the text is still in the current cell.

▼ When Excel cuts off an entry at the right edge of a cell, you can widen that column. But that's a topic best left to Chapter 5.

I've Got Your Number

To type a number, select the cell you want and type a number. For instance, to enter 455 into cell C2, click on cell C2, type **455**, and press Enter.

Checklist

▼ You might think that 89PT100 is a number, but Excel thinks it's text. That isn't a problem unless you want to use the number in a calculation. If you want to use an entry in calculations, it can include only numbers. (How would you add 25 and 37oboe9, anyway?)

▼ Excel aligns numbers to the right edge of the cell. And nothing fancy is displayed—no commas, no currency signs, nothing.

▼ To type a negative number, type a minus sign and then the number.

▼ When the entry is so long that it won't fit into the width of the current cell, Excel displays something like

    1.2E+10

This is *scientific notation*. You must be working on the national debt, because you've got some pretty big numbers. You can widen the column, a trick you learn in Chapter 5.

SCIENTIFIC NOTATION

Scientific notation is a shorthand method of displaying a big number. For example, 1.2E+10 is 1.2 times 10^9 (1 with 9 zeros behind it).

Keeping Track of Dates Every Time

To include dates and times in your worksheets, you just need to type them in a form that Excel recognizes. Excel recognizes lots of different date and time formats.

Excel's Date and Time Formats

Type the date like this	Shorthand	Explanation
4-Apr	d-mmm	day, month
9/23/62	m/d/yy	month, day, and year
23-Sep-62	d-mmm-yy	day, month, and year
Sep-62	mmm-yy	month and year
12:01 AM	h:mm AM/PM	hour, minute, and AM or PM
12:01:00 AM	h:mm:ss AM/PM	hour, minute, second, and AM or PM
12:01	h:mm	hour and minute
12:01:00	h:mm:ss	hour, minute, and second
9/23/62 12:00	m/d/yy h:mm	month, day, year; then hour and minute

Other things to ponder when entering dates and times

▼ You can include the slash (/) or hyphen (-) character as part of an entry, as in 1/23/93 or 23-Jan-93.

▼ No matter what format you use to enter the date, Excel stores it in the format m/d/yy.

▼ Excel converts your entry into a serial number. This number represents the number of days from the beginning of the century until the date you type. Doing so enables you to do calculations on dates and to ask that all-important question: "How many days until the next payday?"

▼ Excel converts times to a fraction of a 24-hour day so that you can do calculations on times. How many minutes until lunch?

▼ You can enter dates and times into the same cell, as in the entry 1/23/93 1:35 am. Be sure to separate the date portion from the time portion with a space.

▼ Excel ignores capitalization when you are entering dates and times; therefore, the date 23-JAN-93 is the same as 23-jan-93.

▼ You can enter military times. For example, the entry for eleven o'clock at night is 23:00.

▼ When you include *am* or *pm* as part of a time entry, Excel assumes that you want to use the 12-hour (not the military) clock.

Formulas (Numbers that Think)

Let's face it. Nobody likes talking about formulas. They remind us too much of seventh-grade math, when we had that first "eyes glazing over"

experience. But Excel formulas have nothing to do with nor look anything like the formulas from our algebra/trigonometry/calculus/theoretical particle physics/teenage days. Formulas provide the magic in a spreadsheet!

To enter a formula, click on the cell where you want the result to appear. Then type an equal sign. The equal sign tells Excel that what comes next is a formula. Then type the equation you want and press Enter.

The key to formulas is using cell references. Suppose that cell B1 contains 5 and cell B2 contains 10. You could create a formula like

=5+10

but this isn't any better than a calculator!

Instead, you can tell Excel to use the cell's value, like this:

=B1+B2

Excel will total the numbers in each cell. If you change a number in either cell, the formula automatically updates the answer.

Checklist

▼ Excel displays the correct answer (not the formula you typed) in the cell.

▼ When the cell with the formula is active, you see the formula in the formula bar.

▼ This is just the bare bones of formulas. You'll put formulas through their paces in Chapters 7, 13, and 14.

I HATE EXCEL!

CHAPTER 2

Making Changes
(Quick-Change Artist)

IN A NUTSHELL

▼ Correcting mistakes
▼ Deleting entries
▼ Undoing changes
▼ Selecting a range
▼ Getting help

I HATE EXCEL!

The thrill of using a spreadsheet is the ease with which you can change things. For instance, maybe you thought you were going to sell 200,000 of those "pet sticks," but ended up selling only 2. The business calculations you set up in your worksheet probably need some major adjustments. Or maybe you need to correct a mistake—a typo, a wrong number, a glaring error. Or maybe you want to make changes because you simply changed your mind.

This chapter covers the most common editing changes you can make in a worksheet. And because you're a preferred customer, I've included a section on how to use Excel's on-line help feature, absolutely free!

No, No, No...It's All Wrong!

There are two ways to correct mistakes in Excel. You can correct them as you make them, or you can correct them after you make them. (Microsoft currently is working on a new Excel feature that enables you to correct them before you make them.)

Actually, you might not be fixing mistakes. Maybe you're just "making changes." Yeah, they're not mistakes; they're just changes you need to make.

Fixing While You Work

Whenever you're typing on your keyboard, the stuff you're typing appears in the cell as well as in the formula bar. If you notice a typing mistake and haven't pressed Enter yet, you can make a change before you

put the entry into the cell. Just press Backspace to delete up to the point where you want to make the change. Then type something new and improved.

Fixing after the Fact

If you press Enter, the entry is already made, and you'll have to use a different procedure to change it.

If you want to replace an entry with something entirely new—like changing that budget entry from *Ferrari* to *Volkswagen*—make that cell the active one, retype the information, and press Enter.

If you want to slightly change the entry—like changing that budget entry from *Trip to Spain* to *Trip to Scranton*—you can edit the cell by using a different method.

First, select the cell you want to change, then click the mouse button or press F2. The insertion point appears in the formula bar, where you can make changes. You are now in Edit mode. (The status bar reminds you of this by displaying *Edit*.)

To accept the new, edited version of the cell, press Enter. To go back to the original entry, don't press Enter. Press Esc instead.

BUZZWORDS

INSERTION POINT

The insertion point is the vertical line that moves while you're typing in the formula bar. It indicates where the text that you type will appear.

▼ Press the left- or right-arrow key to move the insertion point left or right, respectively, one character at a time.

▼ Press Home to quickly move the insertion point to the very front of the entry.

▼ Press End to quickly move the insertion point to the very end of the entry.

▼ Press Backspace to delete the character to the left of the insertion point.

▼ Press Del to delete the character to the right of the insertion point.

When you're finished making changes, press the Enter key. Or click on the check mark button (☑) at the left end of the formula bar.

To cancel the whole exercise so that nothing gets entered into the active cell, press the Esc key. Or use the mouse to click on the X button (☒) at the left end of the formula bar.

Deleting Entries

Sometimes you just want to get rid of the entry entirely. To completely erase the contents of a cell, make that cell the active one, and then press the Del key. When Excel displays the Clear dialog box, click on the All button and then click OK.

TIP

Press Ctrl+Del to skip the Clear dialog box and delete the active cell's contents pronto.

Undoing Changes

(Going back in time)

In Excel, you can undo things that you've just done in a worksheet! You can go back in time as if it never happened. Typed over an important formula? You can undo it. Deleted a really important number? You can undo it. Lost a fortune in the stock market crash of '87? Well, Excel's Undo feature is great, but not that great.

To undo something, open the Edit menu and choose the Undo command. Excel undoes the last thing you did, presenting you with the worksheet as it looked before your boo-boo. For example, if you made something bold by mistake, choose the Undo command to undo it.

TIP

Read this if you don't know how to choose a menu command:

Excel displays nine menu names in its menu bar. Each menu offers a unique grouping of commands. To open a menu, place your mouse pointer on its name in the menu bar and click the mouse button once. If you're a keyboard fanatic, hold down the Alt key and press the underlined letter in the menu name. For example, press Alt and E to open the Edit menu.

TIP

Excel "pulls down" the menu, revealing an assortment of commands. To choose a command, point and click on the command name with your mouse. Or, from the keyboard, press the underlined letter in the command name. If you decide not to choose a command after all, press Esc twice.

Checklist

▼ To even be able to have a shot at successfully undoing something, you must use the Undo command immediately after you screw up, and absolutely before you do a single other thing. You can only undo the last thing you did.

▼ Although Excel can undo most things in a worksheet, there are a few things that it simply never will be able to handle, such as recovering a worksheet you accidentally deleted or making a work-sheet look like it did five days ago at precisely 4:32 in the afternoon.

▼ The description for the Undo command in the Edit menu constantly changes to reflect the action you just took in the worksheet. For example, after you type an entry into a cell, the Edit menu entry says Undo Entry, but after you use the Del key to erase an entry from a cell, the Edit menu says Undo Clear.

▼ Excel doesn't warn you when you've taken an action in the work-sheet that can't be undone. The only way you'll know is when you open the Edit menu and see the Can't Undo message, which means that you're out of luck.

▼ You can quickly undo something by pressing Ctrl+Z, the shortcut key for the Undo command.

▼ The most destructive thing you can do in Excel that simply cannot be undone with Undo is deleting a file with the File Delete command. (More on this one in Chapter 4.)

▼ Every blue moon or so, you'll do something in the worksheet that requires more memory than the Undo feature can handle. Before Excel actually completes this "something," it'll display an alert box warning you that Excel will be unable to undo the event should you choose to proceed. Click No if you want to cancel the activity. If you want to continue the operation, knowing full well that you won't be able to undo it if you need to, click Yes.

Selecting a Range

(Target practice)

When you edit a worksheet, it's much faster to select all the stuff you want to work with, then execute a command. For instance, if you want to delete several cells, don't select and delete and select and delete and so on, deleting each cell individually. Instead, select all the cells and delete them all at once.

A selection of cells is called a *range* and is identified by a *range address*. The *range address* is the top left cell in the range, a colon, and the bottom right cell in the range. For instance, the range A1:B2 includes these cells: A1, A2, B1, and B2.

▼ To select a range with the mouse, click on the cell at one corner of the range and drag to the opposite corner.

▼ To select a range with the keyboard, hold down the Shift key and use the arrow keys to highlight the range.

▼ To select an entire row, click on the row letter.

▼ To select an entire column, click on the column letter.

▼ To select the entire worksheet, click on the blank rectangle at the top of the row numbers and to the left of the column letters.

▼ To select cells that aren't next to each other, click on the first cell. Then point to the next cell you want to select. Hold down the Ctrl key and click the mouse button. Continue Ctrl-clicking until you select all the cells you want.

Once you've selected a range, you can do lots of things to all the cells in that range: format them, change their alignment, copy or move them, delete them, and so on. The command you choose is applied to each cell in the range.

To deselect a range, click anywhere outside of it.

Getting Help

(It's only an F1-call away)

As you work in Excel, you might reach a situation where you just don't know what to do. Excel can talk you through many problem situations, swiftly and painlessly.

Whenever you need help with anything in Excel, press the F1 key. Excel displays a general help contents window that lists information about everything from *Microsoft Product Support* to *Switching from Multiplan* (whatever that means).

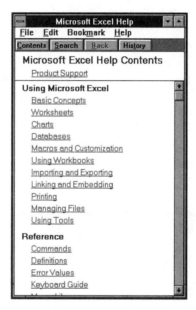

A general help
window in Excel

To choose a topic, look for the green and/or underlined word that corresponds to that topic, and then click on it with your mouse. A second list of topics appears. Click on the subtopic you want; a more detailed help window with an explanation of the selected topic appears.

▼ You can scroll line-by-line through any help window with your mouse or keyboard. With a mouse, click on the up or down scroll arrows at the right edge of the help window; with your keyboard, press the up- or down-arrow key. Use the PgUp or PgDn keys to scroll through the help window one window at a time.

continues

I HATE EXCEL!

CHAPTER 2

▼ To redisplay the main help window from any other help window, click on the Contents button.

▼ When the help you need can be phrased in the form of a how-can-I question, like "How can I move around a worksheet?" start by selecting the help topic called *Basic Concepts*.

▼ To move back to the previous help window, click on the Back button.

▼ To exit help and return to your worksheet, open the File menu from the help window and choose the Exit command. Keyboard maniacs can press Alt+F4.

BUZZWORDS

CONTEXT-SENSITIVE HELP

Excel also offers context-sensitive help. This type of help displays a help window that relates exactly to what you were doing the moment you pressed F1.

Best of all, you don't have to go traipsing through lots of topic windows just to get a simple answer to a simple question. (Remember asking mom how to spell a word, and being told to look it up in the dictionary?) For instance, suppose that you open a menu and aren't sure what a command does. Use the arrow keys to highlight the command. Then press F1. Excel displays a help window that relates to that exact command.

TIP

Most Excel dialog boxes also contain a Help button. Click the Help button to get the same context-sensitive help window.

CHAPTER 3
Saving and Exiting
(File Shenanigans)

IN A NUTSHELL

▼ Saving a worksheet

▼ Saving new stuff in an old worksheet

▼ Changing the name of a worksheet

▼ Turning off the Excel program

All the effort you put into a worksheet goes for nothing if you don't save the worksheet. Saving the worksheet ensures that your hard work is tucked away where you can work on it again. This chapter covers the all-important task of saving. After you save, you're free to go—yes, exit Excel and turn off the computer.

Save It or Lose It

(Tough love with your worksheets)

Whenever you stick a file folder into your briefcase, you do so with the expectation that the next time you open the briefcase, the folder will still be there. But imagine opening the file folder, expecting to see that beautiful report with the cool, color graphs you made, only to find the file folder completely empty.

The one thing you're sure to hate about Excel (and any software program for that matter) is that it's not smart enough to know when it should make a permanent copy of your hard work. An Excel worksheet won't become permanent until you tell Excel to make it permanent. The worksheets you create on-screen are temporary and can easily be lost if there's a sudden power failure, if you turn off your computer, or if you exit the program.

To make a permanent record of a worksheet, you must "save" the worksheet. To save the worksheet means to take the worksheet and store it on your computer's hard disk. (It isn't called a hard disk because it's hard to find, but because it's inside a hard metal box that sits inside your computer.) Your computer's hard disk is your "electronic briefcase." As soon as you save your worksheet, you'll be able to retrieve it from your electronic briefcase as often as you like.

Saving Your Worksheets

(From certain doom)

Get into the habit of saving your worksheets at regular intervals during your workday. If you save regularly, you'll never have to experience the pain of re-creating a worksheet that's accidentally been lost. For really important work, saving every few minutes or so wouldn't be out of the question. Here's how to save a worksheet:

1. Open the File menu and choose the Save command.

The first time you save a worksheet, Excel will display the Save As dialog box.

Type a file name here

SHEET1 is a temporary name that Excel gives the worksheet. Excel fully expects you to come up with a better one. The name you choose should be more distinctive so that you'll be able to tell your worksheets apart.

2. Type a name, like BUDGET93.XLS.

This name has two parts to it: BUDGET93 is the first name and XLS is the last name (called the *extension*). A period separates the

two. You can use up to 8 characters for the first name and 3 characters for the last. Also, don't use any blank spaces, and avoid using punctuation in your worksheet names.

3. Click OK.

As soon as you click OK, Excel names your worksheet and saves it on your hard disk. The new name now appears in the worksheet's title bar.

Checklist

▼ Every worksheet must have a first name (of up to eight characters), but you don't have to type the last name. When you leave off the last name, Excel adds the last name XLS. For instance, the file name MONEY becomes MONEY.XLS. (The letters *XLS* stand for *ex-el-spreadsheet.*)

▼ Excel does not accept more letters than are allowed in a file name. Try using the name EGGSBENEDICT and an alert box appears. Click OK and supply a shorter name.

▼ Choose first names that describe the worksheet's information.

▼ When typing a name, you can use either uppercase or lowercase characters. It makes no difference.

▼ Whenever the name you type for a new worksheet already belongs to another worksheet, Excel displays the message: `Replace exist-ing 'NODOUGH.XLS'`? (in this example, you're trying to create a second worksheet named NODOUGH.XLS). Click on the Cancel button to stop. Excel returns you to the Save As dialog box. Now type a unique name.

▼ The quickest way to save a worksheet is to click on the Save tool in the toolbar. It's the third icon from the left and looks like a floppy disk. Keyboard enthusiasts can press Shift+F12 to do the same thing.

▼ Excel keeps your worksheets in very specific locations on your hard disk. Unless you tell Excel otherwise, it saves the file to the current directory, which is listed at the top of the Save As dialog box. To put the file in a different directory, you must change to that directory. If you aren't sure how to change directories, you need to get your hands on the companion book *I Hate Windows*.

BUZZWORDS

FILE

A file is a collection of data you want to record permanently on your computer's hard disk. In the case of Excel, the data collection happens to be in a worksheet. In word processing programs they're in documents, and in database programs they're in, well, databases.

BUZZWORDS

DIRECTORY

A directory is a section of your hard disk set up to store certain types of files. Similar to a folder, a directory keeps all files in an easy-to-find spot. A directory can also contain other directories. Sometimes the term "subdirectory" is used to refer to directories within directories, but basically directory and subdirectory mean the same thing. Only one directory can be current at a time.

Saving the Second Time, Third Time, and So On

The Save As dialog box appears on-screen only the first time you save a worksheet. This box appears so that you can name the worksheet. Every other time you save the same worksheet by using the File menu's Save command, Excel assumes that you want to keep using the same name, so it doesn't bother with the dialog box.

CAUTION

As you work on your worksheet, keep in mind that the changes you make aren't recorded (saved) until you save the worksheet on-disk again. The disk version includes only the changes you made up to the last time you saved.

Every time you save a worksheet after you've saved it the first time, Excel does very little to show that the worksheet's actually being saved. Scary, huh? Here are a couple of road signs you can keep an eye out for when saving your worksheets.

▼ Try watching your computer (not the screen, but the box itself) as you save a worksheet. Most computers show a red, blinking light when they're saving a worksheet to the hard disk.

▼ Try listening to your computer as you save a worksheet. Most computers make a chirping, whirring sound when they're saving a worksheet to the hard disk. Sounds sort of like a squirrel that's had ten cups of coffee.

▼ Look at the very left end of the formula bar. Excel displays a progress message here while it saves your worksheets. The problem is that today's computers are pretty darn fast, so this message may appear and disappear in the blink of an eye.

Changing a Worksheet's Name

(Excel's witness-protection program)

Do you hate the name you just gave to your worksheet? You can save it with a new name.

TIP

Saving a file with a new name is also handy when you want to have two similar versions of a worksheet. Save the worksheet with a new name to create a copy of that worksheet. You can make any changes you want to the copy; the original is still intact in its original form.

Open the File menu and choose the Save As command. Keyboard junkies can press F12 instead. As soon as you choose this command, Excel displays the Save As dialog box. (Yes, it's the same dialog box you get when you use the Save command on a worksheet for the first time.) Notice that the current worksheet name is highlighted below "File Name" in the dialog box.

Type a new name and click OK. As soon as you click OK, Excel saves a copy of your worksheet, using the name you typed. For now, you have two versions of the same worksheet, each with a different name, on your hard drive.

Closing Worksheets and Exiting Excel

(Until another day)

If you're like me, you look forward to turning off your computer at the end of the day. It's the office worker's equivalent of the factory whistle.

Unfortunately, computers make few notable sounds when you turn them off. In fact, things get even more quiet—that is, unless a colleague down the hall accidentally turns off his or her computer before saving stuff and exiting Excel. Then you'll hear that factory whistle blow.

CAUTION

> Before you exit Excel or turn off your computer, save your worksheet. Before you turn off the computer, exit both Excel and Windows.

To exit Excel, open the File menu and choose the Exit command. Excel disappears from your screen. You are returned to the Program Manager (Windows).

If you forget to save your worksheet, Excel reminds you with an alert box. Click Yes to save the worksheet and then exit. Click No to discard (throw away, ignore, toss out, forget for eternity) all the changes you've made and exit. Click Cancel to return to the worksheet to do whatever.

To exit Windows, open the File menu and choose the Exit Windows command. When you see an alert box that asks whether you are sure you want to exit, click on OK. You are returned to a blank screen with something like C:\> at the top. Now you can turn off your computer.

CHAPTER 4

Opening, Closing, and Deleting Worksheets

(File Shenanigans II)

IN A NUTSHELL

▼ Opening a worksheet
▼ Closing a worksheet
▼ Getting a new, blank worksheet
▼ Deleting a worksheet

This chapter covers even more useful stuff you can do to your worksheets. Things like opening the worksheet you were using the last time you ran Excel and getting a fresh, blank worksheet so that you can create something new and exciting. And for the adventurous, you'll see how to dispose of those old, worn-out worksheets you no longer need.

Opening an Existing Worksheet

(Picking up where you left off)

Naming worksheets and saving them on your hard disk is the equivalent of labeling file folders and stuffing them into your briefcase. This section explains how to reach back into your "electronic briefcase" and pull out your file folders.

When you save a worksheet, you store the information in a file, and you store the file on your computer's hard disk. When you want to continue working with that same worksheet at a later date, perhaps to type in a few more numbers or change a title, you must reopen it in Excel.

Here's how to open a worksheet:

1. Open the File menu and choose the Open command. Excel displays the Open dialog box.

Type the name of the file you want here ——

Or click on it in —— this file list

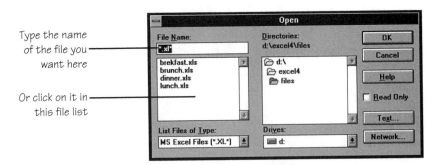

Notice the highlighted text underneath File Name in this dialog box. The mysterious *.xl* is a coded message that tells Excel what types of files to display below. Decoded, *.xl* means "all Excel files."

2. Find your worksheet name in the files list and click on it once.

Its name pops into the File Name box. If you'd prefer to type the name instead, go ahead.

3. Click OK. Excel opens the worksheet and displays it on-screen.

You can combine steps 2 and 3 by double-clicking on the worksheet name in the files list.

TIP

If the worksheet you want to open is one of the last four that you opened, try this shortcut: Click on the File menu. At the bottom of the menu, you'll see a list of the last four worksheets that were opened. Click on the one you want.

Checklist

▼ You can have more than one worksheet open at once. If you have a worksheet open and then open another, they both appear on-screen. The one you opened most recently is on top and is the *active* worksheet. (You can tell an active worksheet by its title bar—it appears in a different color.) See Chapter 12 for the gymnastics of working with more than one worksheet at a time.

▼ Keyboard devotees can press Ctrl+F12 to quickly display the Open dialog box.

continues

▼ When the worksheet you type in the File Name box doesn't exist, Excel displays a message saying so. Click OK to continue. Try again, but this time pick from the file list.

▼ When typing the name of the worksheet you want to open, you can use either uppercase or lowercase characters. It makes no difference to Excel.

▼ To open a file that's stored in a different directory, you must change to that directory. If you aren't sure how to change directories, you need to get your hands on the companion book *I Hate Windows*.

▼ When you try to open a worksheet that's already open on-screen, Excel displays a message such as `Revert to saved BRUNCH.XLS?` (This message appears if you're trying to open a worksheet named BRUNCH.XLS that's already open.) Click the Cancel button to stop.

EXPERTS ONLY

What's wild about wild cards?

In DOS espionage circles, the secret code *.XL* contains "wild cards." Just as a wild card in poker can match any card, a wild card in Excel can match any character or characters. When you see *, it means "insert whatever you want here." So the code *.XL* means "look for all files with any first name, but whose last name uses X and L for the first two characters and anything for the third character." This code would locate the files BRUNCH.XLS, LUNCH.XLM, and SUPPER.XLC if they existed.

EXPERTS ONLY

Wild cards are really useful for narrowing the number of files that displays in the Open dialog box.

To use a wild card, open the File menu and choose the Open command. Type the wild card into the File Name box and click OK. Excel immediately displays a list of the matching files. The following table displays some examples of how you can use wild cards in your day-to-day Excel work.

.	Displays all file names in the current directory
*.XLS	Displays Excel worksheet names only
DINNER.*	Displays all files whose first name is DINNER, as in DINNER.XLS, DINNER.DOC, and DINNER.YUM
LUNCH*.XLS	Displays all worksheets whose first name begins with the word LUNCH, as in LUNCH91.XLS, LUNCH92.XLS, and LUNCH93.XLS

TIP

To quickly open a worksheet, click on the Open tool in the toolbar. It's the icon second from the left that looks like an open folder. When the Open dialog box appears, double-click on the worksheet name in the file list.

Closing a Worksheet

(I'm done for now)

It's a good idea to close worksheets you aren't working on. Open worksheets take up memory and crowd your electronic desktop (your

screen). If you are working on a worksheet and want to close it (put it away), save the worksheet first. Then open the File menu and choose the Close command. Keyboarders can press Ctrl+F4 to do the same thing.

Getting a Fresh New Worksheet

(Starting from scratch)

You've created a worksheet and saved it. Now you're ready to start creating another one. But where does Excel keep all its spare worksheets? To display a new, blank worksheet on-screen, open the File menu and choose the New command. Excel displays the New dialog box. The word *Worksheet* is highlighted.

Click OK. Excel opens a blank worksheet on-screen. The name of this worksheet says SHEET2 or SHEET3 or something similar to that. Excel uses the same dummy naming scheme for each new worksheet you open into the program. The very next time you start Excel on your computer, though, the first worksheet you'll see will be named SHEET1. If you want to change this dummy name to something more descriptive, take a look at "Changing a Worksheet's Name" in Chapter 3.

TIP

The quickest way to get a new worksheet is to click on the New tool in the toolbar. It's the icon at the very left end of the toolbar and resembles a small worksheet. As soon as you click on this tool, a new worksheet appears on-screen.

Getting Rid of a Worksheet

(Without doing hard time)

Most worksheets eventually outlive their usefulness. Either you no longer need the data, or the worksheet itself is obsolete. Every so often you should draw up a list of worksheets that fit into this category and delete them. If you're sharing your computer with someone else, be sure to check with that person before you delete anything.

When you delete a worksheet, you are actually erasing the information from your hard disk. This procedure is like pulling a file folder from your briefcase and tossing it into the trash. Not only does deleting old worksheets make it easier to manage the ones that remain behind, but it also frees up room on your hard disk for saving new information.

To delete a worksheet, open the File menu and choose the Delete command. As soon as you choose this command, Excel displays the Delete Document dialog box.

Type the name of the worksheet you want to delete here

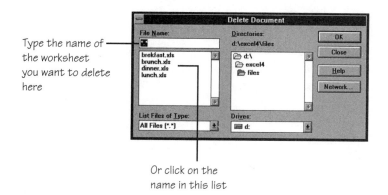

Or click on the name in this list

Excel shows you a complete list of all the files in the current directory. To delete a file that's stored in a different directory, you must change to that directory. (If you aren't sure how to change directories, you should

read the companion book *I Hate Windows*.) When you see the name of the worksheet you want to delete in the list, click on the name. The worksheet name pops into the File Name box. Click OK.

As soon as you click OK, Excel displays a question box asking whether you're sure that you want to delete the file. This is your last chance to change your mind, so think really hard before continuing.

Click on the Yes button to delete the file from your hard disk. After you delete a worksheet, you cannot open it up in Excel ever again, at least not without some special program and the help of a data recovery whiz.

Click on the No button to stop the delete operation dead in its tracks. Excel returns you to the Delete Document dialog box. Choose a different file to delete (the one you meant to pick in the first place) and then click OK. Or click Close to stop this deleting stuff altogether. Excel returns you to your worksheet.

CAUTION

Deleting a worksheet is a long-term commitment. Once a worksheet is gone, it's gone for good. Before you actually consummate the deal, double-check that the file name displaying in the question box is, in fact, the name of the worksheet you want to delete. Also, never delete a file whose name you do not recognize. The unrecognizable file could be one of the many different files that Excel needs to operate correctly, and you don't want to accidentally delete one of them!

"I HATE THIS!"

I accidentally killed my worksheet!

It's happened to everyone at least once. You accidentally delete a worksheet that you really needed after all. If you're lucky, you are friends with an expert who can raise deleted files from the dead. Call and ask for help. The chances for this voodoo succeeding are excellent as long as you do one thing:

THE MINUTE YOU DELETE THE FILE, STEP AWAY FROM YOUR COMPUTER AND GO CALL YOUR FRIEND!

Do not allow anyone near your computer until the cavalry gets there. Tape a piece of paper to the front of your computer, warning everyone to stay away or else.

I HATE EXCEL!

DEADLINE!!

By JEFF MACNELLY

HURRY UP WITH THAT COLUMN!!

RIGHT!...ALMOST FINISHED...

A FEW MORE CORRECTIONS ON THE WORD PROCESSOR...

AND NOW TO ENTER IT INTO THE MEMORY...

GLORP!

WHAT'S WRONG?

I'M HAVING SOME ELECTRONIC PROBLEMS...

WHAT'S THE MATTER WITH THE COMPUTER?

IT THREW UP.

CHAPTER 5

Formatting Your Worksheet

(From Ugly Duckling to Swan)

IN A NUTSHELL

- ▼ Adding bold and italic style
- ▼ Making text bigger and smaller
- ▼ Aligning text and numbers
- ▼ Using different numeric formats
- ▼ Widening columns

All Excel worksheets start out as ugly ducklings. All those words and numbers by themselves do little to inspire the people who read your reports. The best worksheets are accurate and pleasing to the eyes.

Formatting is the key to making a worksheet attractive. You start with a plain worksheet and spiff it up a bit so that your boss, a colleague, or a client says stuff like, "Wow, it's so clear to me now!" and "What a work of art!"

Excel offers you lots of formatting tools—tools that let you widen columns, line up text, and make words bold. This chapter looks at the most popular of these tools.

TIP

Keep in mind that you can open the Edit menu and choose the Undo command (or press Ctrl+Z) to reverse any of the formatting commands you'll test drive in this chapter.

Changing Type Styles

If you make important words and numbers stand out, you can direct a reader's attention to the important stuff first. There are three good ways to make text stand out: make the type bold, make the type italic, or resize the type.

To Boldly Go Where No Type Has Gone Before

You've just finished creating the year-end sales worksheet. The totals are absolutely outstanding. But the numbers just aren't bold enough.

Microsoft Excel

File Edit For**m**ula Format **D**ata **O**ptions **M**acro **W**indow **H**elp

Normal

A1

EOYSALES.XLS

	A	B	C	D	E	F	G	H	I
1									
2									
3		Brash 'n Bold Swimwear							
4		Annual Sales Report							
5									
6				1st Quarte	2nd Quarte	3rd Quarte	4th Quarte	End-Of-Year	
7		One Piece		12,407	8,581	6,199	11,805	$38,992	
8		Bikini		7,301	11,465	10,078	5,623	$34,467	
9		Thong		11,470	12,349	8,481	8,530	$40,830	
10		Dental Floss		11,722	11,621	6,422	11,191	$40,956	
11		Fiber Optic Cable		6,816	6,726	9,502	7,930	$30,974	
12		Totals:		$49,716	$50,742	$40,682	$45,079	$186,219	
13									
14									
15									
16									
17									
18									

Ready

BEFORE:
*Just a boring old
worksheet*

Adding bold to a worksheet is easy. Select the cell that contains the type you want to make bold. Click on the Bold tool in the toolbar. It's the button with the picture of the bold **B** on it. Excel instantly makes the contents of the cell bold. To remove the bold style from your type, just click on the Bold tool again.

Keyboarders can quickly add bold style to the contents of the active cell by pressing Ctrl+B.

TIP

Italic (Text on the slant)

Adding italic style is a subtle way of helping the reader figure out what's what in the worksheet. For example, you might want to make your column headings italic.

 To use italic style, select the cell that contains the type you want to make italic. Click on the Italic tool in the toolbar. It's the button with the picture of the *I* leaning to one side. Excel instantly makes the contents of the cell italic. Do the same for any other cells you want to enhance. To remove the italic style from a cell, just click on the Italic tool again.

TIP

Keyboarders can quickly add italic style to the contents of the active cell by pressing Ctrl+I.

Checklist

▼ There are no laws saying that some type should always be bold and other type should always be italic. It's completely up to you to decide what looks right.

▼ Avoid using bold or italic for all the type in a worksheet—it'll defeat the purpose of using these "discriminating" tools in the first place.

▼ You can also make text both bold and italic. Click both the Bold and Italic buttons in the toolbar (one after another, of course).

▼ If you change the type to bold and italic, but see ######## in the cell as a result, you need to widen the column. You'll learn about that in "Widening Columns," later in this chapter.

▼ The Bold and Italic buttons appear "pushed in" after you click on them the first time. When you remove the style from a cell, the buttons return to their original "pushed out" appearance. Because of this appearance change, you can easily tell when a particular style has been added to (or successfully removed from) the active cell.

▼ To make a bunch of cells bold or italic at once, select the range of cells before you click on the Bold or Italic tool. Chapter 2 explains how to select a range of cells.

Sizing Up Your Type

Changing the size of type in your worksheets is useful for emphasizing and de-emphasizing text. For example, newspapers, magazines, and books all use bigger type for titles and headlines, and smaller type for main body text and footnotes. You can do the same thing in your worksheets.

  Enlarging and shrinking the size of type in a worksheet cell is simple. First select the cell whose type size you want to change. Then click the Increase Font Size or Decrease Font Size tools in the toolbar. They're the two buttons (next to the Italic tool) that contain the letter A. The one with the larger A increases size, and the button with the smaller A decreases size. You can continue clicking on these buttons to achieve even greater increases or decreases in size, but Excel has its limits. When you can no longer affect the size of type in a cell, Excel beeps and nothing happens to the cell.

I HATE EXCEL!

	Microsoft Excel		
<u>F</u>ile	<u>E</u>dit	Formula	Format	<u>D</u>ata	<u>O</u>ptions	Macro	<u>W</u>indow	<u>H</u>elp

Normal

A1

EOYSALES.XLS

	A	B	C	D	E	F	G	H	I
1									
2									
3		Brash 'n Bold Swimwear							
4		Annual Sales Report							
5									
6				*1st Quarte*	*2nd Quart.*	*3rd Quarte*	*4th Quarte*	*End-Of-Year*	
7		One Piece		12407	8581	6199	11805	**38992**	
8		Bikini		7301	11465	10078	5623	**34467**	
9		Thong		11470	12349	8481	8530	**40830**	
10		Dental Floss		11722	11621	6422	11191	**40956**	
11		Fiber Optic Cable		6816	6726	9502	7930	**30974**	
12		Totals:		**49716**	**50742**	**40682**	**45079**	**186219**	
13									
14									
15									
16									
17									

Ready

HUH?

BUZZWORDS

FONT

Computer programs use the word "font" to describe unique families of type and all their possible sizes. For instance, Courier is one font family and Arial is another. Windows comes with several built-in fonts, which are available to you in Excel. What I've referred to as "type size" is more accurately described as a font's "point size." The word "point" refers to an age-old measurement system that examines the height of a single character in terms of points. One point is equal to 1/72 inch.

To return the contents of a cell to its original size, click the Increase Font Size or Decrease Font Size button until the type size returns to the way it was before you changed it.

TIP

> The quickest way to remove all special styles you've added to the contents of a cell—including bold style, italic style, and point-size changes—is to make that cell active and press Ctrl+1.

Displaying Numbers That Make Sense

When you enter numbers into cells, you can see that Excel displays the numbers pretty much the way you type them. The number 45.5 appears as 45.5 and the number 2903 appears as 2903. But not all numbers are created equal. If you don't think so, consider accepting payment for a debt owed to you in gallons instead of dollars. This example shows why it's so critical that your worksheet numbers make sense.

One way to show what a number means is to type a text description, such as "pounds" or "days," near the number in the worksheet. A more useful technique is to apply one of Excel's built-in *number formats* to improve the number's appearance.

Follow these steps:

1. Select the cell or range of cells you want to format. Selecting a range is covered in Chapter 2.

2. Open the Format menu and choose the Number command. Excel displays the Number Format dialog box.

3. Click on the Category list choice that best describes the number you're formatting. For instance, to format a number to display it as dollars, click on Currency.

As soon as you click on an item in the Category list, Excel displays the formats available for that category in the Format Codes list.

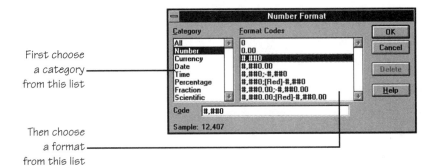

First choose a category from this list

Then choose a format from this list

4. Click on a code style in the Format Codes list box.

"I HATE THIS!"

What the heck is #,###0.00?

Excel uses a cryptic numbering scheme to explain the numeric formats. The easiest way to figure out a particular numeric format is to click on it and then check the sample in the dialog box. If the number looks the way you want it, you've got the format you want.

5. Click OK. Excel applies the number format to the number in the active cell.

TIP

You can either enter numbers the way you want them formatted or use shortcut keys. For instance, if you want the number 1200 shown as currency, either you can type **$1,200** and press Enter, or you can type **1200**, press Enter, and then press Ctrl+$. For percentages, you can type something like **10%**, or you can enter **.1**, press Enter, and then press Ctrl+%.

The Number Format categories explained

▼ The All category displays a comprehensive list of the format codes for all of the following categories.

▼ The Number category displays positive and negative numbers, with or without commas and decimal places. Some examples of this category are 2546 and 2,546 and 2,546.00. Excel can display negative numbers like (2,546) in red on-screen.

▼ The Currency category displays positive and negative dollar values. Excel can display negative numbers in red on-screen.

▼ The Date category displays date numbers in one of five date formats. The most popular formats are 6/15/93 and 15-Jun-93.

▼ The Time category displays time numbers in one of the five time formats. The most popular formats are 12:03 and 12:03:12 AM.

▼ The Percentage category displays numbers as percents, with or without decimal places. Examples of this format include 5.24% and 5%.

continues

The Number Format categories explained, continued

▼ The Fraction category displays numbers as fractions, like 1/4, or mixed numbers, like 2 11/25.

▼ The Scientific category displays numbers in scientific notation. For example, the number 50,000 displays as 5.00E+04.

Goldilocks and the Three Alignment Tools

Excel automatically aligns text at the left edge of a cell and aligns numbers at the right. But these alignments may not work for your worksheet. You might want to use a different alignment. Aligning makes things neat and orderly so that you (and everyone else) can easily read and understand what's in a worksheet.

You can change either of these alignment styles by selecting the cell you want to change and then clicking on one of the alignment buttons on the toolbar:

Button	Name	Purpose
	Left Align tool	Shifts data to the left edge of the active cell
	Center Align tool	Shifts data to the center of the active cell
	Right Align tool	Shifts data to the right edge of the active cell

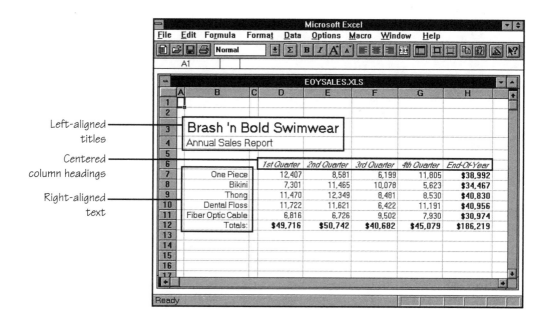

Left-aligned titles — Brash 'n Bold Swimwear / Annual Sales Report

Centered column headings

Right-aligned text

The spreadsheet shows:

	1st Quarter	2nd Quarter	3rd Quarter	4th Quarter	End-Of-Year
One Piece	12,407	8,581	6,199	11,805	$38,992
Bikini	7,301	11,465	10,078	5,623	$34,467
Thong	11,470	12,349	8,481	8,530	$40,830
Dental Floss	11,722	11,621	6,422	11,191	$40,956
Fiber Optic Cable	6,816	6,726	9,502	7,930	$30,974
Totals:	$49,716	$50,742	$40,682	$45,079	$186,219

Widening Columns

There are two occasions when you'll get the urge to widen a worksheet column. The first is when you've entered text into a cell whose neighbor to the right also contains some stuff. As you'll recall from Chapter 2, Excel lops off the tail end of the first entry in such circumstances so that you can't see it anymore. The second is when you've entered a really long number into a cell and all that shows is a whole slew of number signs (########).

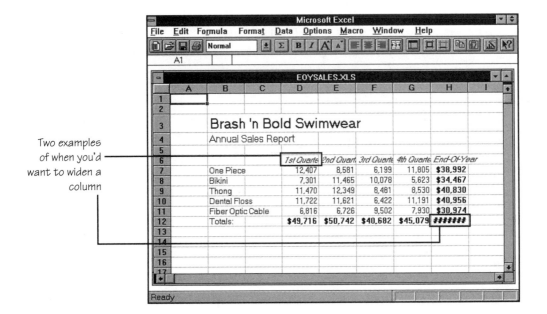

Two examples of when you'd want to widen a column

Excel gives you lots of alternatives when it comes to changing the width of a column. The two most popular of these are using what Excel calls the Best Fit option and dragging the column.

Best Fit (One size fits all)

If you want Excel to figure out how big to make the column (big enough to fit the widest entry, plus a little breathing room), use the Best Fit option:

1. Select any cell in the column you want to widen.

2. Open the Format menu and choose the Column Width command.

Excel displays the Column Width dialog box. You can type a width into the Column Width text box, but if you're not quite used to eyeballing column widths yet, let Excel size the column for you.

3. Click on the Best Fit button.

Excel automatically sizes the column so that it's slightly wider than the contents of the active cell. You can see everything that's in the cell, but the column is not so wide that there are miles of blank worksheet until the next column.

TIP

There's even a quicker way to use the Best Fit option. When you know the column you'd like to use the Best Fit option on, point your mouse pointer at the vertical bar on the right side of the column heading and double-click there. That's it!

Dragging the Column

The other way to widen a column is to drag the column by using your mouse:

1. Point your mouse at the vertical bar next to the column letter for the column whose width you want to change.

Look just underneath the worksheet's title bar to locate the vertical bar. If you intend to widen column B, for instance, you'd move the mouse pointer to the vertical bar between B and C in the column heading. Your mouse pointer changes into a vertical bar that has two opposing arrows: one pointing left and one pointing right.

2. Drag the vertical bar to the right to increase the column width or to the left to decrease the column width.

   To drag the bar, click and hold the left mouse button while your pointer is on the vertical bar, and then move the mouse to the left or right.

3. When the column width is where you'd like it, release the mouse button.

CHAPTER 6

Printing Basics
(Staying between the Lines)

IN A NUTSHELL

▼ Preparing to print
▼ Previewing a worksheet
▼ Printing a whole worksheet
▼ Printing only a few pages in a large worksheet
▼ Stopping a runaway printer

When you've created a worksheet that looks good enough to eat, it's time to think about printing it onto paper. Printing a worksheet creates a permanent work record you can file away, give to a colleague, or turn into an origami masterpiece.

For many, the thought of printing conjures up images of ancient Aztec rituals: pouring out libations of toner and sacrificing paper in the hopes that something (anything!) actually pops out of the printer.

Printing in Excel, fortunately, doesn't require an advanced degree in mysticism. You only need to learn how to use one or two commands to be able to successfully print your worksheets and graphs. This chapter shows you how.

Checking Out Your Printer

(Is it alive?)

Before tackling any printing exercise, check out your printer to see whether it's in good working order. The following items might seem obvious to you, at least until you spend the better part of an afternoon trying to print when the power cord is unplugged.

Important things to look out for before you print

▼ Look behind the printer to see whether the power cord is plugged into the back of the printer and into the wall. If it isn't, plug it in. And make sure that the power cord between the back of the printer and the back of the computer is plugged in at both ends. You might have to wiggle these power cords a little to make sure that there's a good connection. (Cats and small children have a funny way of getting back there and undoing power cords.)

▼ Check out the front of your printer. See whether the printer is turned on and ready for printing. A printer makes a whirring, grinding noise when you first turn it on. Then a series of lights on the front or top of the printer will come on, indicating that your printer is ready to go.

▼ Make sure that the printer has an ample supply of paper. Some printers use paper trays, like copy machines; others use tractor-feed paper, the stuff with hole-punched, tear-away sides. Feed in the paper. If you don't know how, ask someone who does.

▼ Most printers have an On-Line button located near the front or top of the unit. When this button is illuminated, your printer is on-line, which means that it's ready to print. When the On-Line button is not illuminated, the printer is off-line. Printers can't print when they're off-line, so press the button once to put it back on-line before you try to print.

Using Print Preview

(Sneak a peek)

You're ready to print. All the right lights are lit, the cords are plugged in, and you've fed in enough paper to print 500 copies of your worksheet. Even though you're ready to start printing, you're a little bit hesitant. You remember your last printing experience. You printed, and nothing happened. You printed again, but half of your information didn't show up. So you tried a third time, but the printing started halfway down the first page. (Where's that sledgehammer?)

The easiest way to guard against PTPD (post-traumatic printing disorder) is to cure all the annoying problems ahead of time. Start by previewing the worksheet.

With your worksheet active in Excel, open the File menu. Then choose the Print Preview command. Excel displays your worksheet on-screen. (This action may take from two to five seconds, depending on the speed of your computer.) The next thing you'll see on-screen is a simulation of your printed worksheet.

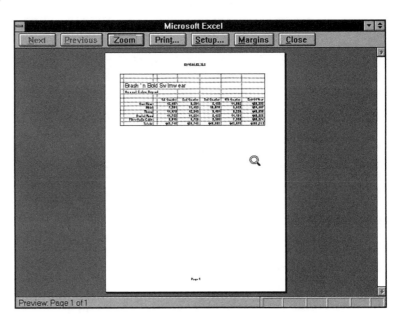

Previewing a worksheet before printing it

Click on the Close button to quit previewing. Excel returns you to the worksheet.

Things you can do while previewing

▼ Press PgUp or PgDn to scroll up or down the worksheet to reveal any information (or pages) that's not showing on-screen.

▼ If you want to magnify an area of the worksheet, click on the Zoom button. You can accomplish the same thing by moving the mouse pointer into the worksheet area, where the mouse pointer becomes a magnifying glass, and clicking once on the part of the worksheet you want to zoom in on.

▼ To change the margins, click on the Margins button. Excel displays a grid over the worksheet. This grid reveals the top, bottom, left, and right margin settings that Excel will use when printing the worksheet. To change a margin, click on the margin line you want to change, and drag it to a new location.

▼ When you're ready to print the worksheet, click on the Print button.

Printing the Whole Thing

(And nothing but the whole thing)

To print a worksheet in its entirety, open the worksheet. Then open the File menu. Choose the Print command. When the Print dialog box appears, click OK. Your worksheet will begin printing within a few seconds.

Notice that Excel provides some other information on the printout. The name of the worksheet file appears at the top. The page number appears at the bottom. Handy.

Here's a quicker way to print a worksheet: With the worksheet open in Excel, click on the Print button in the toolbar. (It's the fourth button from the left and looks just like a little printer.) When the Print dialog box appears, click OK.

Excel handles everything else for you, from deciding where the margins should be to where to start printing a second page for larger worksheets. Sure, Excel allows you to control all of that stuff if you really want to, but for now, who wants to?

Printing Only Part of a Worksheet

You might decide that you need to reprint a couple of pages somewhere in the middle of a long printout, say pages 7 and 8 of a 15-page printout.

To print only a few pages, open the File menu and choose the Print command. When the Print dialog box appears, click on the Pages button inside the Print Range block. The cursor moves into the box labeled From. Type the starting page number, press the Tab key to move the cursor to the To box, and then type the ending page number. Click OK to begin printing the selected pages.

Shooting Trouble

(Right between the eyes)

Ninety-nine percent of the things that can go wrong with printing takes place at the printer, nowhere near your fingers, your computer keyboard, or the sledgehammer you occasionally raise above your head. So when

something does go wrong, don't start banging on the keyboard or hitting buttons on the computer. Remain calm and relaxed, and try a few of the following quick fixes.

How to stop a print operation gone haywire

▼ To cancel a printout before you click OK in the Print dialog box, just click on the Cancel button.

▼ To cancel a printout after you click OK but before your printer starts printing, click on the Cancel button in the Printing dialog box. This dialog box always appears for a moment or two immediately after you click OK to start printing.

▼ To cancel a printout after your printer starts printing, turn off the printer, wait 5 to 10 seconds, and then turn the printer back on. Your printer should spit out one final page and then stop.

I HATE EXCEL!

SEE THAT PILE OF TRASH OVER THERE?

—DON'T TOUCH IT.

LISTEN, IT'S THE NINETIES...

YOU DON'T NEED TO KEEP ALL THIS PAPER ANYMORE.

YOU COULD GET RID OF THIS ENTIRE PILE OF TRASH...

WE HAVE COMPUTERS, YOU KNOW.

I KNOW.

SO WHY DON'T YOU STORE SOME OF THIS ON THOSE LITTLE COMPUTER DISCS?

I DO.

WHAT DO YOU THINK THAT PILE IS?

PART II

Making It Look Good

Includes:

CHAPTER 7

Formulas and Functions
(Doing Work That Adds Up to Something)

IN A NUTSHELL

- ▼ Creating formulas
- ▼ Using cell addresses in formulas
- ▼ Dealing with formula entry problems
- ▼ Using functions, Excel's built-in formulas
- ▼ Using the AutoSum tool

Formulas are the backbone of your worksheets. But as worksheet features go, the formula is the most misunderstood and maligned of them all. Mention this word to computer novices and watch their faces go blank and their eyes roll back into their heads.

In techie terms, a formula is something that uses math symbols to describe a relationship between numbers. A formula can be something as simple as this:

$$10 + 5 = 15$$

or something as bizarre as this:

$$\delta\theta = \tfrac{1}{2}(\delta x + \delta y) + \tfrac{1}{2}(\delta x - \delta y)\cos 2\theta + \tau xy \sin 2\theta$$

In *your* terms, formulas are equations that answer questions like "What's 10 plus 5?" or "What's the average of these 12 sales totals?" or "Just how much money does Uncle Sam take from me?"

What's a Formula Look Like?

(Give me some useful examples, please)

The most basic kind of Excel formula looks a lot like the calculations you'd scribble on a piece of paper when figuring out your paycheck. Note the following classic example:

$$750 - 200 = 550$$

This formula says that your total pay minus the government's cut equals the cash you can stick in your pocket. To enter that information into an

Excel worksheet, pick any cell in your worksheet, and then type this formula

=750–200

and press Enter. As soon as you press Enter, Excel displays the value 550 in the cell. Now look up in the formula bar. Your formula is still there. Excel stores formulas in cells exactly as you type them, but shows the answer in your worksheet.

Checklist

▼ Excel formulas always start with the equal sign. The equal sign tells Excel to show you the answer.

▼ Occasionally you'll slip and type a formula in a form that resembles the handwritten, cocktail-napkin variety, such as 750–200=. When you type a formula this way, Excel won't show you an answer. As far as Excel is concerned, the entry 750–200= is text, because you didn't start by typing an equal sign.

▼ Avoid typing blank spaces in formulas. Even though you can use blank spaces in many kinds of formulas (just like the ones you write out on paper), leaving the spaces out of the formulas you type into worksheet cells makes things look cleaner.

▼ There are six math symbols you can use to tell Excel which math operation to perform. The plus (+) symbol means add; the minus (–) symbol means subtract; the asterisk (*) symbol means multiply; the slash (/) symbol means divide; the caret (^) symbol means raise to the power of; and the percent symbol (%) means divide by 100.

▼ Formulas can do more than one math operation at a time. Just string together the numbers you want to calculate. The formula =5+32*120–345/12 performs four different math operations. Can you spot them all?

BUZZWORDS

EXPONENTIATION

The math operation that uses the caret (^) symbol is commonly known—that is, among astrophysicists and nuclear engineers—as "exponentiation" (ex-pah-nen-chee-ay-shun). The rest of us call this operation "raising something to the power of something else." You can use this operation to figure out how your personal finances would be affected if your weekly salary of $750 were squared. The Excel formula that calculates the answer (but sadly fails to produce the additional cash) is =750^2.

Creating Smarter Formulas

(Cell addresses and pointing techniques)

Of course, there's more to creating formulas than typing an equal sign and a few numbers. You'll eventually want to create formulas that calculate with lots of numbers all over your worksheets. The smartest Excel formulas use the addresses of cells that contain values, rather than the values themselves. And you can create formulas in ways that are more efficient than typing formulas into the formula bar.

Showing Up at the Right Address

Suppose that you've entered our sample paycheck formula into a worksheet. Your supervisor comes by and tells you that starting next

week, your payroll taxes will increase by $23.52 per week. Now you have to edit the formula so that it looks like this:

=750–223.52

This change is easy enough to make when you are dealing with a couple of short formulas. But what happens when you have to change 50 formulas every other day during your work week? Ouch! To make these changes easier, create a formula that references values you have typed into your worksheet. For example, imagine that you've typed your total pay number into cell A5 and your total taxes number into cell A6. You could now type the formula

=A5–A6

into cell A7. Again, Excel displays the answer to the formula in the cell where you typed it, cell A7 in this case. If your payroll taxes go up, just type the new amount into cell A6. The boss gave you a weekly raise of $200? Enter that new value into cell A5. Each time you change one of the values that's referenced in the formula, Excel calculates a new answer in cell A7. That's the thrill of an electronic worksheet.

It's Okay To Point

Okay. You've figured out that it makes much more sense to use cell addresses in your formulas. The next trick is to point to the cell rather than type the address. For instance, suppose that you want to total up each month's sales dollars in the following worksheet.

I HATE EXCEL!

	A	B	C	D	E	F	G	H	I
1									
2		The Media Revolution							
3		Monthly Sales Report							
4									
5			Jan	Feb	Mar	Apr	May	Jun	
6									
7		Record	3,268	3,200	2,538	4,246	9,425	2,939	
8		CD	6,180	7,864	8,791	8,762	12,314	6,336	
9		Cassette	2,050	587	1,413	1,262	4,080	1,426	
10		Video	2,351	2,784	4,914	6,203	4,614	4,392	
11		Total:							
12									
13									
14									
15									
16									
17									

Microsoft Excel — RECORD.XLS — C11 — Ready

File   Edit   Formula   Format   Data   Options   Macro   Window   Help

The formulas will go in row 11, starting in cell C11

Follow these steps:

1. Click on cell C11 to make it the active cell. This is where you want to put the formula for January's total sales.

2. Type the equal symbol (=) to start the formula.

3. Click the mouse pointer inside cell C7, the first cell address you want to put in formula.

   A rotating outline appears around the cell you clicked. Excel then copies the address for cell C7 into the formula bar next to the equal sign. You've just pointed out the first cell address!

TIP

> Keyboard lovers can press the arrow keys to select the cells they want.

4. Type the plus (+) symbol so that Excel knows to add numbers.

The rotating outline disappears from cell C7. The original cell, C11, again becomes the active one.

5. Click the mouse pointer inside cell C8, the next cell address you want in your formula.

The rotating outline appears again, this time around cell C8. Excel copies the address for cell C8 into the formula bar next to the plus sign. You've just pointed out the second cell address!

6. Repeat steps 4 and 5 until the cell addresses for C9 and C10 are included in the formula bar.

7. Press Enter.

Excel enters the formula into cell C11 and displays the answer: 13,849. You can use this same technique to create formulas for the other blank cells in this worksheet, cells D11 through H11.

The formula entered into cell C11

The formula's answer

	A	B	C	D	E	F	G	H	I
1									
2		The Media Revolution							
3		Monthly Sales Report							
4									
5			Jan	Feb	Mar	Apr	May	Jun	
6									
7		Record	3,268	3,200	2,538	4,246	9,425	2,939	
8		CD	6,180	7,864	8,791	8,762	12,314	6,336	
9		Cassette	2,050	587	1,413	1,262	4,080	1,426	
10		Video	2,351	2,784	4,914	6,203	4,614	4,392	
11		Total:	13,849						
12									
13									
14									
15									
16									
17									

Microsoft Excel — RECORD.XLS
C11 =+C7+C8+C9+C10

TIP

For a fast method of entering the same formula into other cells, copy it. See Chapter 9 for information on how to do this.

HUH?

BUZZWORDS

MARQUEE

The proper terminology for that rotating outline is "marquee," just like the flashing, neon marquees you see around movie theater signs.

Home, Home on the Range

In some formulas, you want to work on a range (a selected group of cells). Chapter 2 covers ranges in more detail, but here are some key range facts:

BUZZWORDS

CELL RANGE

"Cell range" is one of the top 10 Excel catch phrases you should never forget. In worksheet hacker's lingo, a cell range is a shorthand way to describe a group of cells. A range can be one cell, a column of cells, a row of cells, or any other block of cells.

Checklist

▼ The most common way to select a range is to click and hold down the mouse button on the first cell you want to include (the top left cell of the range). Then drag the mouse to the last cell you want to include (the range's bottom right cell). Release the mouse button. Go back and read Chapter 2 if you want to know other methods of selecting a range.

▼ Ranges are useful when you want to sum a group of cells.

▼ Ranges, like cells, are designated with a shorthand address. The first cell address describes the cell in the top left corner of the group, and the second cell address describes the cell in the bottom right corner of the group. For example, B2:C4 is a range that includes the cells B2, B3, B4, C2, C3, and C4.

I HATE EXCEL!

	Microsoft Excel						

File Edit Formula Format Data Options Macro Window Help

Normal

C11   =C6+C7+C8+C9+C10

RECORD.XLS

	A	B	C	D	E	F	G	H	I
1									
2		The Media Revolution							
3		Monthly Sales Report							
4									
5			Jan	Feb	Mar	Apr	May	Jun	
6		*Laser Disc*	987	1,022	1,422	981	2,221	1,099	
7		*Record*	3,268	3,200	2,538	4,246	9,425	2,939	
8		*CD*	6,180	7,864	8,791	8,762	12,314	6,336	
9		*Cassette*	2,050	587	1,413	1,262	4,080	1,426	
10		*Video*	2,351	2,784	4,914	6,203	4,614	4,392	
11		Total:	14,836						
12									
13									
14									
15									
16									
17									

A selected range

Ready

Changing Your Address

(Editing cell addresses in formulas)

Not surprisingly, editing a formula is just like editing anything else in the formula bar, and you use all the same keys and techniques. In addition, when you're editing a formula in the formula bar, you can continue pointing out new cell addresses to add to the formula.

Suppose that you've added another category to the sample record store worksheet. The new information appears on row 6, just above the Record category. Typing in the new numbers is a start, but for your formula answers to be on the mark, you'll have to edit them to include this new row of information.

Make cell C11 the active cell. Press F2 to enter Edit mode. Excel shifts the contents of the cell into the formula bar for editing. The cursor appears at the right end of the formula.

Type a plus (+) to tell Excel that you're continuing the formula. Click the mouse pointer inside cell C6. Excel copies the address for cell C6 into the formula bar next to the plus sign.

Excel adds cell address C6 to the formula

The marquee appears after you click inside cell C6

	Microsoft Excel							

File Edit Formula Format Data Options Macro Window Help

Normal

C6   =+C7+C8+C9+C10+C6

RECORD.XLS

	A	B	C	D	E	F	G	H	I
1									
2		The Media Revolution							
3		Monthly Sales Report							
4									
5			Jan	Feb	Mar	Apr	May	Jun	
6		Laser Disc	987	1,022	1,422	981	2,221	1,099	
7		Record	3,268	3,200	2,538	4,246	9,425	2,939	
8		CD	6,180	7,864	8,791	8,762	12,314	6,336	
9		Cassette	2,050	587	1,413	1,262	4,080	1,426	
10		Video	2,351	2,784	4,914	6,203	4,614	4,392	
11		Total:	9+C10+C6						
12									
13									
14									
15									
16									
17									

Point

Press Enter. Excel refigures the formula and shows the new answer in cell C11. Notice that the cell addresses don't have to be in any particular order in a formula. You can type **C6** at the beginning of this formula (instead of at the end), and Excel will calculate the correct answer. Excel doesn't care about the order of appearance of the cell addresses in most formulas, as long as they're all there.

A Formula's Pecking Order

Suppose that you want to add the numbers 50 and 2, and then multiply that answer by the number 100. Doing the math in your head, you quickly come up with the right answer: 5200. But when you type the formula =50+2*100 into a cell, Excel displays 250 as the answer.

What gives? Excel has a strange way of looking at formulas that combine two or more different math operations—in this case, addition and multiplication. It may seem strange, but Excel is actually following a fundamental rule of math. This rule says that certain math operations, like multiplication and division, are always performed before other math operations, like addition and subtraction. The order goes like this:

▼ Math operations in parentheses ( ) are always performed first

▼ Exponentiation (**^**) operations are performed second

▼ Multiplication (*****) and division (**/**) are performed third

▼ Addition (**+**) and subtraction (**–**) are performed last

You might be wondering how the heck you can enter a formula which, first, is supposed to add some numbers and then, second, multiply the answer by another number? The trick is to use parentheses. You can use parentheses to set apart special math operations. Excel always performs the math inside a pair of parentheses before it does the math outside of the parentheses. If you enter the formula as **=(50+2)*100**, Excel will do the addition before the multiplication.

Formulas That Go Bump in the Night

Whenever Excel can't make heads or tails of a formula you're trying to type into a cell, it keeps your formula in the formula bar and displays a

dialog box that describes the problem. These dialog boxes say things like `Error in formula` and `Parentheses do not match`. When you can see what's wrong in your formula, click on the OK button. Excel returns you to the formula bar.

How to fix a formula

▼ If Excel has an idea of what went wrong, it'll highlight that part of your formula for you, which makes it easier to edit the formula. Type the correct part and press Enter.

▼ If Excel can't figure out exactly what's wrong, it highlights the entire formula bar. Press the Home key to move the cursor to the beginning of your formula. Now make the necessary corrections in the formula. When you're finished correcting the formula, press Enter to store the formula in the active cell.

▼ When you can't see what's wrong with your formula, try clicking the Help button. Excel displays a Help window that contains a list of the most common kinds of formula entry boo-boos. Hopefully, yours is on this list. When you're finished getting help, open the File menu and choose Exit (or press Alt+F4 to exit quickly). Excel returns you to the error message dialog box. Go ahead and fix the problem.

▼ When you can't spot the problem in the formula bar and the Help window is no help at all, it's best to start all over again. Click OK in the dialog box and then click the X button in the formula bar or press the Esc key. Excel cancels your formula and returns you to Ready mode. Try writing out the formula on paper before retyping it into the worksheet. This procedure might help you figure out what went wrong.

Error Message Blues

Occasionally Excel still might have problems with a formula you've typed into a cell. When Excel is unable to properly calculate the formula and display an answer for you, it displays a rather odd-looking error message inside the cell. You're most likely to encounter one of the following messages during your formula-entry escapades.

Error Message	What It Means
#DIV/0!	You're attempting to divide by 0, the cardinal sin of mathematics. (Fall to your knees and beg forgiveness from Pythagoras.) To correct the formula, remove the part that divides by zero. If it's a reference to a cell address that contains zero, edit that cell instead of the formula.
#NAME?	No, Excel doesn't want to know what your name is. This message is telling you that you misspelled a function name, or you typed a formula that contains a cell name Excel doesn't recognize, as in the formula =C4+BOB.
#NUM!	Don't worry. Excel isn't suffering from hypothermia. This message means that the answer to your formula is a monster-sized number that Excel can't handle, like the national debt figure. Or you typed a function with an unacceptable argument. (Arguments are covered later in this chapter.)

Error Message	What It Means
#REF!	This message means that your formula contains a reference to a cell that has been deleted from the worksheet. (A ten-yard penalty, according to most refs.) Edit your formula by typing a new cell address for the deleted one or by typing the value you want to calculate with.
#VALUE!	It's Excel's half-year clearance sale, and everything's half off! What a value! Actually this message means that you typed a cell range (like C5:C10) when Excel was expecting a single cell address (like C5). Either that or the cell that's being referenced contains text instead of the number Excel was expecting. Edit the formula by typing a single cell address or placing a value in the cell that your formula is referencing.

What's a Function, and What Does It Look Like?

Functions are time-saving tools you can use to simplify math in your worksheets. Excel offers hundreds of these built-in formulas, which you can use in place of many of your own worksheet formulas. (See Chapter 13 for a list of the most popular functions.) For instance, rather than creating a formula that adds the values in five consecutive cells, you can use the SUM function instead.

Here's a formula written the old way: **=45+23+65+90+12**

Here's a better way to write this formula: **=A1+A2+A3+A4+A5**

Here's the best way, using a function: **=SUM(A1:A5)**

The Arguments for Using Functions

Except for the familiar old equal sign, Excel's functions look quite a bit different from the standard formula fare. All that other stuff—the function name, the parentheses, and the stuff inside the parentheses—plays an important part in making your functions work properly.

Parts of a function

▼ The function name is a short (sometimes abbreviated) word that generally describes the function's duty. For example, the SUM function sums things for you, and the AVERAGE function averages things for you.

▼ The parentheses are used to separate the function name from the information you want the function to use in its calculation. For example, in the function =SUM(A1:A5), the stuff in parentheses tells Excel which worksheet cells contain the values to be summed.

▼ The *arguments*, which I just unceremoniously called "the stuff in the parentheses," can be values separated by commas, as in =SUM(250,345,129); cell addresses separated by commas, as in =SUM(A1,A2,A3); or a cell range, as in =SUM(A1:A5).

Entering a Function

Using the sample record store worksheet as an example, you can create a
SUM function instead of using the formulas you created in row 11 in the
last exercise. Here's how:

1. Click on the cell in which you want to enter the function. For
example, click on cell C11.

2. Type the equal symbol (=) to start the formula.

3. Type **SUM** and then type a left parenthesis.

4. Drag your mouse through the range of cells you want to sum.
For example, start by clicking in cell C6 and dragging down to
cell C10.

*A rotating outline
appears around
the entire cell
range, and Excel
copies the cell
range into the
formula bar, next
to the left
parenthesis*

	Microsoft Excel							▼ ◆

File Edit Formula Format Data Options Macro Window Help

C6   **X √**   =sum(C6:C10

RECORD.XLS

	A	B	C	D	E	F	G	H	I
1									
2		The Media Revolution							
3		Monthly Sales Report							
4									
5			Jan	Feb	Mar	Apr	May	Jun	
6		Laser Disc	987	1,022	1,422	981	2,221	1,099	
7		Record	3,268	3,200	2,538	4,246	9,425	2,939	
8		CD	6,180	7,864	8,791	8,762	12,314	6,336	
9		Cassette	2,050	587	1,413	1,262	4,080	1,426	
10		Video	2,351	2,784	4,914	6,203	4,614	4,392	
11		Total:	um(C6:C10						
12									
13									
14									
15									
16									
17									

Point

5. Type a right parenthesis to complete the function.

The rotating outline disappears from the cell range. The original cell again becomes the active one.

6. Press Enter.

Excel enters the function into the cell and displays the answer.

TIP

Whenever Excel can't make heads or tails of a function you're trying to type into a cell, it reacts the same way as it does when it doesn't recognize a formula. For help with your functions, refer to the section "Formulas That Go Bump in the Night," earlier in this chapter. It covers formula-entry problems.

Warp Speed Addition with the AutoSum Tool

 Excel includes a tool that automatically sums a range of cells for you, to save you even more time! To use this feature, select the cell where you'd like the SUM function to appear. Next, click on the AutoSum tool in the toolbar. It's the one to the left of the Bold tool and contains the Greek letter sigma (Σ).

As soon as you click on this tool, Excel inserts the SUM function into the formula bar. Excel takes a guess at the numbers you want to sum and shows the marquee around that range. To accept that range of cells and store the function in the active cell, click OK. If you want to sum a different range of cells, highlight the cell range with your mouse and then press Enter.

CHAPTER 8

Editing
(Messing with Your Worksheet)

IN A NUTSHELL

▼ Repeating worksheet operations
▼ Inserting rows and columns
▼ Clearing cell entries
▼ Deleting rows and columns
▼ Learning special editing techniques

This chapter covers valuable worksheet editing techniques. Did you forget one of the lines in your row of figures? See how to insert a row or column. Want to get rid of a cell? Learn how to delete it. Step right up and see all this and more in the amazing worksheet editing chapter. Right here. Right now.

Repeating History

You've seen how easy it is to undo mistakes you make in Excel worksheets. Just choose the Edit Undo command. For those who can't get enough of the things you do *right* in your worksheets, there's the Edit Repeat command. With this command you can actually repeat the things you've just done in a worksheet.

Changed the font for a cell range and now you'd like to add the same font to a different cell range? You can repeat it quickly. Aligned a whole column of text and now you want to do the same for another column? You can repeat that quickly, too. Made a large deposit into your bank account? Hah, now wouldn't that be a great trick?!

To repeat your last command, move to a place in the worksheet where you want the activity repeated; then open the Edit menu and choose the Repeat command. For example, suppose that you've just added a fancy font to cell range D5:K5. To apply the same font to a different cell range, say C125:P125, select that range and choose the Edit Repeat command.

TIP

You also can quickly repeat a worksheet activity by pressing Alt+Enter, the shortcut key for the Edit Repeat command.

▼ Until you perform some other worksheet activity that's repeatable, you can repeat your most recent worksheet activity as many times in a row as you want.

▼ The description for the Repeat command in the Edit menu constantly changes to reflect the action you just took in the worksheet. For example, after pressing Del to clear an entry from a cell, the Edit menu entry will say "Repeat Clear." If you used the Format Font command to change the font for a cell, the Edit menu will say "Repeat Font."

▼ You can't use the Repeat command to repeat stuff you've typed into a cell. To accomplish this task you have to either retype the information elsewhere or copy it. (You'll learn how to copy in the next chapter.)

▼ Excel doesn't warn you about worksheet activities that can't be repeated. The only way you'll know is when you open the Edit menu and see the "Can't Repeat" message. At this point, unfortunately, you're plum out of luck.

Inserting More Space in a Worksheet

Everyone who creates Excel worksheets eventually finds the need to insert blank rows and columns. Sometimes you just need to add an extra category or two. Rather than typing the new information in the bottom row or in the column farthest to the right, you can insert a blank row or column and type the new data exactly where you need it.

Inserting Rows and Columns (Move over)

You've just finished typing in the information for a new worksheet report—let's call it the Weekly Production Schedule. As you admire your fine work, you suddenly notice that you left out two important categories of data. You forgot to include a column for the Saturday schedule, and you left out the row where the Gadgets data belongs.

The Weekly Production Schedule worksheet report

	Microsoft Excel									
File Edit Formula Format Data Options Macro Window Help										

	A	B	C	D	E	F	G	H	I	J
1										
2	FussBudget Manufacturing									
3	Weekly Production Schedule									
4										
5		Mon	Tue	Wed	Thu	Fri	Sun			
6	Fidgets	300	427	152	922	976	234			
7	Fudgets	75	696	78	967	294	345			
8	Gidgets	311	510	758	950	968	567			
9	Widgets	881	22	915	758	30	678			
10	Wudgets	173	182	619	142	662	789			
11	Total	1,740	1,837	2,522	3,739	2,930	2,613			
12										
13										
14										
15										
16										
17										
18										

PRODUCE.XLS

Ready

In the sample worksheet, you need to insert a blank column between F and G, and you need to insert a blank row between 7 and 8. This will save you the trouble of having to retype worksheet data to make room for the missing categories.

The quickest way to insert a row or column is to select the entire row(s) or column(s) where you want to insert blank space, and then choose Edit Insert. (To select an entire row or column, click on the number in the row heading or the letter in the column heading.) When you insert a

row, Excel pushes down the row where the active cell was, leaving a single, blank row in its place. When you insert a column, Excel pushes the active column to the right, leaving a single, blank column in its place.

	Microsoft Excel
File Edit Formula Format Data Options Macro Window Help	

A1

| PRODUCE.XLS |

	A	B	C	D	E	F	G	H	I	J
1										
2	FussBudget Manufacturing									
3	Weekly Production Schedule									
4										
5		Mon	Tue	Wed	Thu	Fri		Sun		
6	*Fidgets*	300	427	152	922	976		234		
7	*Fudgets*	75	696	78	967	294		345		
8										
9	*Gidgets*	311	510	758	950	968		567		
10	*Widgets*	881	22	915	758	30		678		
11	*Wudgets*	173	182	619	142	662		789		
12	*Total*	1,740	1,837	2,522	3,739	2,930		2,613		
13										
14										
15										
16										
17										
18										

Inserted column —

Inserted row —

Ready

"I HATE THIS!"

I hate it when there are 50 ways to do the same thing!

You also can use the Insert dialog box to insert blank rows and columns wherever you need them in your worksheet. Instead of selecting the entire row or column, position the active cell anywhere in the row or column where you want to insert new data. Open the Edit menu and choose the Insert command. In the Insert dialog box, click on the Entire Row option or the Entire Column option, and then click OK.

EXPERTS ONLY

I only want to insert part of a row or column

To insert a partial row, use your mouse to highlight the cell range where you want to insert new data, such as cell range D10:H10. Open the Edit menu and choose the Insert command. In the Insert dialog box, click on the Shift Cells Down option and then click OK. Excel pushes down only those cells in the columns you highlighted, leaving a blank partial row in its place. Cell range D10:H10 shifts down to cells D11:H11, D11:H11 shifts down to D12:H12, and so on.

To insert a partial column, use your mouse to highlight the cell range where you want to insert new data, such as cell range G5:G15. Open the Edit menu and choose the Insert command. In the Insert dialog box, click on the Shift Cells Right option and then click OK. Excel pushes to the right only those cells in the rows you highlighted, leaving a blank partial column in its place. Cell range G5:G15 shifts over to cells H5:H15, H5:H15 shifts to I5:I15, and so on.

TIP

To insert more than one blank row or column at a time, highlight two or more cells in a row or column before you choose the Edit Insert command.

To undo any insert operation, immediately choose the Edit Undo command or press Ctrl+Z.

What Happens to Your Formulas?

When it comes to inserting rows and columns, Excel treats your worksheet formulas with kid gloves. That's because your formulas use cell addresses. And when you insert rows or columns, these same formulas might try to use numbers from cells that are now blank. Fortunately, when you do insert rows or columns, Excel generally adjusts all affected formulas so that they continue pointing to the same cells, even though they are at different cell addresses.

Let's see how this works. To help you understand how formulas change when you insert rows and columns, refer to the sample worksheet shown here as you read the following checklist.

Cell B12 is highlighted to show you an example of the formulas in row 12

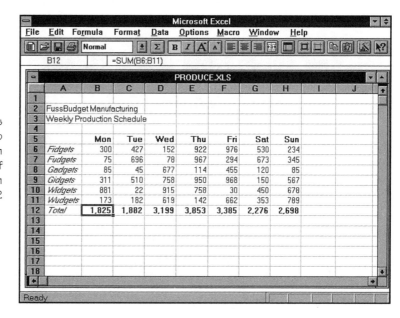

▼ Let's say that you insert a new column to the left of column B. Column B now becomes column C. Excel changes all formulas to reflect their new column positions. For example, the formula in B12 moves to C12 and changes from =SUM(B6:B11) to =SUM(C6:C11). All other columns are affected in the same way.

▼ If you insert a new row above row 6, row 6 becomes row 7. Excel changes all formulas to reflect their new row positions. For example, the formula in B12 moves to B13 and changes from =SUM(B6:B11) to =SUM(B7:B12). All other rows are changed as well.

Deleting Space from a Worksheet

Once you're comfortable inserting blank rows and columns, you're ready to move on to something much more exhilarating: deleting entire rows and columns! Now before you start haphazardly deleting stuff from a worksheet, let me say this one thing: always be wary when it comes to deleting stuff. When you delete a row or column, you delete all the entries in that row or column. Are you sure you don't need anything? Are you sure that you're sure?

TIP

If you want to rearrange the worksheet—move some entries to another spot—you don't have to delete the entries from one spot and reenter them in another. You can move them. The next chapter explains how to move stuff.

To recover from a delete operation, immediately choose the Edit Undo command or press Ctrl+Z.

Clearing Cells (To make room for new prisoners)

Let's start small and see the quickest way to delete information from just a few cells. Start by selecting a few cells in your worksheet. Then open the Edit menu and choose the Clear command. As soon as the Clear dialog box appears, click OK. Poof! Your cell data disappears.

TIP

To skip the Clear dialog box, just select the cells you want to delete and press Ctrl+Del. The cells are cleared.

What about the four mysterious options inside the Clear dialog box? Do they mean anything important?

Options in the Clear dialog box

▼ The All option erases the contents, formatting, and notes from the cells you selected.

▼ The Formats option erases only the formatting from the cells (like number formats or bold), leaving the contents and notes intact.

▼ The Formulas option erases only the contents of the selected cells, leaving the formatting and notes intact.

▼ The Notes option removes notes from the cells you selected, leaving the contents and formatting intact.

Deleting Rows and Columns (Out of my way!)

Suppose that it's now six months later. Your supervisor just announced that the manufacturing plant is scaling back production. The Saturday and Sunday shifts have been eliminated. And those geniuses over in

CHAPTER 8

marketing have decided to scratch Fudgets and Widgets from the product line. You quickly open your Weekly Production Schedule in Excel and begin assessing the damage.

As usual there are two ways to proceed. First, you can type the whole darn thing over again. Second, you can selectively delete columns and rows from your worksheet.

The quickest way to delete a row or column is to select the entire row or column (click on the number in the row heading or the letter in the column heading). Then choose Edit Delete. When you delete a row, Excel removes everything in that row from the worksheet, pulling up the row beneath that one to fill the empty space. When you delete a column, Excel removes everything in that column and pulls over the column to the right to fill the empty space.

The sample worksheet after deleting the target rows and columns

	Microsoft Excel										

File Edit Formula Format Data Options Macro Window Help

`Normal` | Σ | B | I | A | A' | ...

A1

PRODUCE.XLS

	A	B	C	D	E	F	G	H	I	J
1										
2	FussBudget Manufacturing									
3	Weekly Production Schedule									
4										
5		Mon	Tue	Wed	Thu	Fri				
6	*Fidgets*	300	427	152	922	976				
7	*Gadgets*	85	45	677	114	455				
8	*Gidgets*	311	510	758	950	968				
9	*Wudgets*	173	182	619	142	662				
10	*Total*	869	1,164	2,206	2,128	3,061				
11										
12										
13										
14										
15										
16										
17										
18										

Ready

"I HATE THIS!"

You mean there's another way to delete them?

Yes, there are two ways to delete rows and columns. Position the active cell anywhere in the row or column you want to delete. Open the Edit menu and choose the Delete command. In the Delete dialog box, click on the Entire Row option (for rows) or the Entire Column option (for columns). Then click OK.

EXPERTS ONLY

Getting rid of only part of a row or column

To delete a partial row, use your mouse to highlight the cell range you want to delete, such as cell range D10:H10. Open the Edit menu and choose the Delete command. In the Delete dialog box, click on the Shift Cells Up option and then click OK. Excel removes the contents of the selected cell range and pulls up only those cells below the ones you highlighted. Cell range D11:H11 shifts up to replace D10:H10, D12:H12 shifts up to replace D11:H11, and so on.

To delete a partial column, use your mouse to highlight the cell range you want to delete, such as cell range G5:G15. Open the Edit menu and choose the Insert command. In the Insert dialog box, click on the Shift Cells Left option and then click OK. Excel removes the contents of the selected cell range and pulls to the left only those cells to the right of the ones you highlighted. Cell range H5:H15 shifts left to replace G5:G15, I5:I15 shifts left to replace H5:H15, and so on.

TIP

To delete more than a single row or column at a time, highlight two or more cells in a row or column before you choose the Edit Delete command.

What Happens to Formulas?

As with inserting rows and columns, deleting them might affect worksheet formulas that use cell addresses. But when it comes to deleting, you must pay closer attention to how the formulas might be affected. In many cases, Excel will adjust the affected formulas so that they continue pointing to the same numbers. Other times, deleting rows and columns will put your formulas on the fritz, like when a formula is trying to calculate with numbers in a row you just deleted. (See Chapter 7 for a list of the most common formula error messages and how to correct the offending formula.)

Checklist

▼ If you delete column B, Excel shifts to the left all the data and formulas from columns C on. All formulas are adjusted to reflect their new location. For example, if you had a formula in column C12 that said =SUM(C6:C11), it would move to B12 and change to =SUM(B6:B11). This applies to rows, too.

▼ If you delete a row or column and that row or column is referenced in a formula, the formula is updated. (That value is no longer included in the result.)

▼ If you delete a row or column that contains formulas, the formulas disappear.

Other Exciting Editing Techniques

If you run into a special editing circumstance—for instance, you need to select all cells in a worksheet that contain a formula, or you have to replace all instances of the word *Widget* with *Midget*—look through this section. The remainder of this chapter looks at several editing techniques.

Moving Somewhere Fast

Are you in a hurry to edit a worksheet, but can't seem to find the cells you're looking for? Do you nod off while scrolling down a worksheet with PgDn, only to discover that you passed your stop minutes ago? If this sounds at all like you, you'll be happy to know that Excel can get you where you're going. And fast, too.

To move to any single cell in a worksheet, open the Formula menu and choose the Goto command. Keyboard nuts can press F5, the shortcut key for the Formula Goto command. When the Goto dialog box appears, type the address of the cell you'd like to visit. Then click OK. Whoosh! Excel moves you there in a flash.

Selecting Specific Types of Cells (picky, picky)

The boss just handed you a worksheet you've never seen before. It takes 35 minutes for Excel to open it. Yep, it's a monster of a worksheet. Three thousand lines of numbers, text, and formulas. Your job? Make a list of every cell in the worksheet that contains a formula; that way, your boss doesn't have to hunt around the worksheet every time it needs updating. The active cell is A1, and there's steam rising from the top of your head.

No problem! With the Formula Select Special command, you can have Excel instantly highlight areas of your worksheet that have unique qualities, like only cells that contain formulas, only cells that contain text, the last cell in the worksheet, and much more.

To use this editing tool, open the Formula menu and choose the Select Special command. Check the option in the Select Special dialog box that describes the type of information you're looking for. Then click OK to turn Excel loose on your worksheet.

Options in the Select Special dialog box

▼ The Constants option selects all cells that contain uncalculated numbers and/or text when the Numbers and/or Text boxes are also checked.

▼ The Formulas option selects all cells that contain formulas.

▼ The Blanks option selects all cells that contain nothing; you know, blank cells.

▼ The Last Cell option selects the last cell in the worksheet that contains data or that's now blank but at one time contained data.

▼ The Objects option selects all graphs you've added to the worksheet. (Graphs are covered in Chapter 15.)

The remaining Select Special options are designed for more advanced editing tasks, such as when you're calculating the median flight speed of the space shuttle while it's traveling backward through a meteor shower.

Finding Information

If you know that somewhere in your worksheet you used the word *noodle* and you want to find it, you can use the Formula Find command to find the cell. The Formula Find command lets you search through a worksheet for specific words, numbers, and formulas.

To use the Find command, follow these steps:

1. Open the Formula menu and choose the Find command.

Excel displays the Find dialog box. It's in here that you can tell Excel all about the stuff you want to find. For most of your find operations, the default settings in this dialog box will work just fine.

BUZZWORDS

DEFAULT SETTINGS

Default settings are the settings that Excel uses unless you tell it otherwise. Most of the time, Excel "guesses" right with the defaults, so you don't need to change any of the options.

2. In the Find What text box, type the text or formula you're searching for, and then click OK.

Excel selects the first cell that contains a match. Press F7 to find the second occurrence, then again to find the third occurrence, and so on. Once you find the stuff you're looking for, what do you do with it? Well, you can edit the entry, retype new stuff into the cell, or delete it completely.

When Excel can't find the stuff you're looking for, it'll display a dialog box message that says "Could not find matching data." Click OK to return to the worksheet. Try again.

▼ You also can press Shift+F5, the shortcut key for the Formula Find command, to display the Find dialog box.

▼ The "Look in" options search for stuff only in certain types of cell entries. Your cell entry choices are Formulas, Values, and Notes. Use Look in Formulas to find cell references, like to find all formulas that reference C5. Use Look in Values to find the calculated values, like to find all cells that have a value of 6. Use Look in Notes to find information in your notes, which are memos you can add to cells.

▼ The "Look at" options search for stuff as a whole or as a part of a bigger entry. For instance, if you're searching for the letters *idg*, the Part option allows Excel to locate the words *Fidgets*, *Widgets*, and *Gidgets*. If you are looking for the word *the* by itself, click on the Whole option, which tells Excel to stop only on the word *the*, not *theater*, *theme song*, or anything else with the letters, *t-h-e*.

▼ The "Look by" options tell Excel how to search through your worksheet, either by rows or columns. Using the production schedule as an example, you would use Look by Rows to look for something by product. To look for something by days of the week, use Look by Columns.

▼ Click on the Match Case check box to locate exact uppercase and lowercase matches for the search text. If you type **pig**, Excel will find *PIG*, *pig*, *Pig*, *piG*, and so on. If you type **pig** and click on Match Case, Excel will find *pig*. It won't stop on *PIG*, *Pig*, or *piG*.

Replacing Information (Tit for tat)

The Formula Replace command can search through a worksheet for specific words, numbers, and formulas and then replace each occurrence with something entirely different. Suppose that your product name has changed from *Widgets* to *Tidbits*; you can change all instances of *Widgets* to *Tidbits* in a flash.

To use the Replace command, follow these steps:

1. Open the Formula menu and choose the Replace command.

Excel displays the Replace dialog box. It's in here that you can tell Excel all about the stuff you want to find and replace. For typical replace operations, the default settings in this dialog box work just fine.

The Match Case, Look at, and Look by options work exactly the same here as they do in a find operation.

2. In the Find What text box, type the stuff you're searching for, such as **Widgets**.

3. In the Replace With dialog box, type the replacement stuff; for example, type **Tidbits**.

4. Click on the Find Next button.

I HATE EXCEL!

▼ After Excel finds the first occurrence of the stuff you're looking for, click on the Replace button to replace the search text with the replacement text.

▼ To find the next occurrence of the search stuff *without* replacing the first occurrence, click on the Find Next button. You can click on this button for each occurrence of the search text you want to skip.

▼ Click on the Replace All button to replace every occurrence of the search stuff with the replacement stuff. Excel does not stop at each occurrence; it blasts through the entire worksheet until the job's done.

▼ To stop the replace operation and return to your worksheet, click on the Close button.

▼ When you accidentally replace something in the worksheet, use the Edit Undo command as soon as Excel returns you to your worksheet.

▼ When Excel can't find the stuff you're looking for, it'll display a dialog box message that says "Could not find matching data." Click OK to return to the worksheet. Try again.

TIP

Excel automatically searches your entire worksheet during find and replace operations—that is, unless you want to do otherwise. To tell Excel to search through only a particular cell range, select the cell range before you choose the Formula Find or Formula Replace command.

CHAPTER 9

Moving and Copying Data
(Rearranging Your Cells)

IN A NUTSHELL

- ▼ Moving cell data
- ▼ Copying and pasting cell data
- ▼ Copying formulas
- ▼ Filling data
- ▼ Pasting special data
- ▼ Switching columns and rows around

When you first start pecking away in your worksheet, you probably aren't going to remember every little fact and figure. And you probably aren't going to get everything in the right cell without some shuffling.

One way to rearrange your worksheet is to insert a new row or column. This trick, covered in the preceding chapter, is great if you left out a row or a column. But what if the change isn't so neat and tidy? What if you want column A where column B is and column C where column A is? Do you have to redo the worksheet? Nope. You can move cells around so that they're where you want them.

A more powerful companion to moving cells is copying them. For example, Excel allows you to enter a formula once and copy it across the row or column, and you can enter the first date and have Excel fill in all the rest. This chapter focuses on ways to rearrange your data.

Moving Cell Data

Creating worksheets is an inexact science at best. You type something into one cell, then decide it doesn't belong there. Instead of erasing the cell's contents and retyping the entry elsewhere, just move it. You can move data by dragging and dropping or by using the menu commands.

Dragging and Dropping (with your mouse)

One way to move stuff is called "dragging and dropping." You literally drag one or more cells to a different area in the worksheet and drop

them there. This method requires a keen eye and a steady hand because you have to make precise mouse pointer movements. (No shaky hands allowed.)

Here's how it works. Suppose that you want to move a cell range like B12:E12 up a few rows to B7:E7. Start by highlighting the cell range you want to move. Then position your mouse pointer anywhere on the thick border that surrounds the selected cell range. The pointer changes from a cross to an arrow when you position it correctly. Now drag the cell range to row 7 and drop it there. And that's how you use dragging and dropping to move cells from one place to another.

Dragging range
B12:E12 up to
range B7:E7

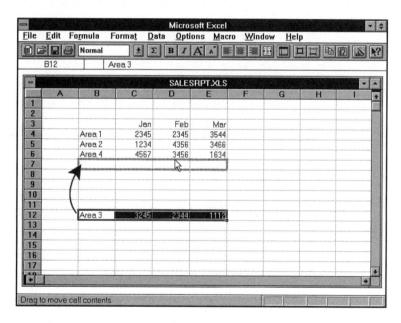

As soon as you release the mouse, the outline border you were dragging disappears, and Excels displays the moved data at its destination.

▼ If you are unable to drag and drop in your worksheets, the Cell Drag and Drop feature is probably turned off. To fix this problem, open the Options menu and choose the Workspace command. Click on the Cell Drag and Drop check box (put an X in it) to enable the feature, and then click OK to return to the worksheet. You may now drag and drop to your heart's delight.

▼ Be sure that you don't drop the cells onto cells that already contain data. The cells you drop will overwrite any stuff in the "receiving" cells. Excel will warn you when this is about to happen.

▼ If you make a mistake, open the Edit menu and choose the Undo command.

▼ If you move a formula or any cells referenced in a formula, all references are adjusted accordingly. You don't have to mess with the formulas at all. Pretty neat, huh?

Cutting and Pasting (with your keyboard)

You also can use your keyboard to move stuff around in a worksheet. Excel calls this particular task "cutting and pasting." The procedure is similar to cutting an article out of a newspaper and taping it onto a piece of paper.

Start by highlighting the cell range you want to move. Next, open the Edit menu and choose the Cut command. Excel displays the marquee around the cell range. Now select the top left cell of the area where you want to move the range. Open the Edit menu and choose the Paste command.

CAUTION

Be sure that you don't paste the new cells over cells that contain data. The pasted cells will overwrite any data in the receiving cells, and you won't get a warning.

Time-saving keystrokes for moving cell data quickly

▼ Press Ctrl+X, the shortcut key for the Edit Cut command, to cut a range of selected cells.

▼ Once you're at the destination spot in the worksheet, press Ctrl+V, the shortcut key for the Edit Paste command. Or you can just select the destination cell and press Enter to paste the cell range.

▼ Press Shift+Del to delete the contents of the selected range. Immediately move to the destination cell range and press Shift+Ins to restore the deleted information in the new location.

▼ Press Ctrl+Z immediately to reverse a move operation.

EXPERTS ONLY

Dropping data between the cracks

If you want to cram cells between existing data, you can try a little trick. You can insert a range of cells—including its data—between existing cells. Highlight the cell range you want to cram, and position the mouse pointer on the range's outline border. Drag the outline border until it's positioned over a row or column, and then press and hold the Shift key. As soon as you press the Shift key, the outline border changes into a thin, horizontal line (for rows) or vertical line (for columns). If the border doesn't change on your screen,

EXPERTS ONLY

slide your mouse around until it does. When the line is properly positioned, release the mouse button. Excel instantly inserts the cell range and pushes the other cells up, down, right, or left, depending on where you stuck the new cells.

Copying and Pasting Cell Data

Copying information is definitely on the list of top 10 most used Excel features. Copying stuff in a worksheet is just like moving it, except that you're actually making a duplicate of something instead of shifting it around the worksheet. Copying data, especially formulas, is a great time-saver. You don't have to type the same thing over and over and over.

Excel offers two ways to copy data in your worksheets: the drag-and-drop method and the menu commands method.

Dragging and Dropping (à la mouse)

Yes, this is the same dance step covered earlier in the chapter. Only here it applies to copying stuff, not moving it. With this feature, you can literally drag a copy of a cell range and drop it into a different area in the worksheet.

Here's how it works. Suppose that you need to create a table for second-quarter sales data, a table that looks almost exactly like another one in your worksheet, except that the numbers and column headings need to change slightly. You can be a total Excel bonehead and type the new information into the existing table, or you can work smart by making a copy of the table and then editing it a little so that you can use it for the second-quarter sales data.

Start by highlighting the cell range you want to copy. Then position your mouse pointer anywhere on the thick border that surrounds the cell range. The pointer changes from a cross to an arrow when you position it correctly. Now press and hold the Ctrl key and drag the cell range to where you want the copy. As soon as you release the mouse and Ctrl key, the outline border you were dragging disappears, and Excel displays the copied data in its destination.

Copying cell
range B3:E7 to
range B9:E13

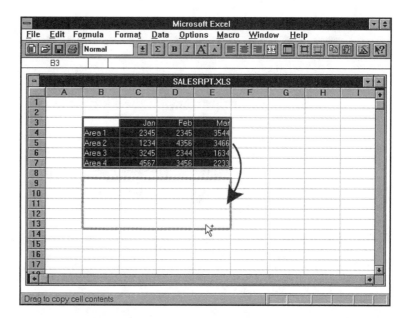

Checklist

▼ There's a tell-tale sign that you're copying a cell range rather than moving one. As soon as you press the Ctrl key and begin dragging a cell range, Excel displays a tiny plus symbol (+) next to the mouse pointer. Whenever you lose track of whether you're moving or copying a cell range, look to see whether the plus symbol is on-screen.

continues

▼ If you drag the copy onto cells that already contain data, the copy overwrites that data, so be careful. Excel will warn you when this is about to happen.

Copying and Pasting (à la keyboard)

You also can use your keyboard to copy stuff in a worksheet. Excel calls this particular procedure "copying and pasting." It's like photocopying a newspaper article and taping the copy to a piece of paper.

Start by highlighting the cell range you want to copy. Next, open the Edit menu and choose the Copy command. Excel displays the marquee around the cell range you're copying. Now select the top left cell of the area where you want to copy the range. Open the Edit menu and choose the Paste command. Excel transfers the copy to the cell range.

CAUTION

Be sure to paste the copy in a blank area. If you select an area of the worksheet that contains entries, the copy overwrites those entries.

Shortcuts you can use when copying cell data

▼ Press Ctrl+C, the shortcut key for the Copy command, to copy a range of selected cells.

▼ Once you're at the destination spot in the worksheet, press Ctrl+V—the shortcut key for the Edit Paste command—to copy

the selected cell range. Or you can just move to the destination cell and press Enter to paste the cell range immediately.

▼ Press Ctrl+Ins to copy the contents of a selected cell range. Immediately move to the destination cell range and press Shift+Ins to transfer the copied information to the new location.

▼ Press Ctrl+Z immediately to reverse a copy operation that goes bust or when you accidentally overwrite other cell data that you need.

▼ You also can copy worksheet data by using the Copy tool in Excel's toolbar. Select the cell range you want to copy, and click on the Copy tool. It's the tool at the right end of the toolbar and shows two documents slightly overlapping one another. Select the top left cell of the area where you want to place the copy, and press Enter.

EXPERTS ONLY

Making room for the copy

If you want to copy cells and cram them between existing data, you can try a little trick. Select the cell range you want to copy, and position the mouse pointer on the range's border. Drag the outline border until it's positioned over a row or column, and then press and hold the Shift and Ctrl keys. As soon as you press these keys, the outline border changes into a thin, horizontal line (for rows) or vertical line (for columns). If the border doesn't change on your screen, slide your mouse around until it does. Position the line where you want to insert the copied range, and then release the mouse button. Excel inserts the cell range and pushes the other cells up, down, right, or left, depending on where you stuck the new cells.

I HATE EXCEL!

EXPERTS ONLY

Be sure that you keep holding down the Ctrl and Shift keys until you release the mouse button. If you happen to release either of these keys before releasing the mouse button, you'll actually be telling Excel to copy your cell range on top of whatever data you happen to be above at the time. Excel displays the message `Overwrite non blank cells in destination?` Click on the Cancel button and try again.

Copying Formulas

(Building worksheets the easy way)

Excel is pretty darn smart when it comes to copying formulas. Consider the formula SUM(C6:C10), which sums numbers in column C. When you copy this formula one cell to the right, Excel changes the copied formula so that it looks like this: SUM(D6:D10).

Notice that only one thing changed in the copied formula—the column letter. Since you placed the copy of the formula in column D, Excel changed the cell addresses so that the formula adds numbers in column D. If you copied the formula into column G, its column letter would change to G.

Can you see how easy it is to create new formulas simply by copying them from cell to cell? Consider what happens when you copy the formula SUM(C6:F6) into a cell one row down. Instead of changing the column letter Excel changes the row number. The copied formula is SUM(C7:F7).

The reason Excel adjusts the formula is because Excel uses *relative references* for the cells. Suppose that you have a formula in cell B5 that sums

the cells in B2:B4. Rather than tell Excel to copy the specific cells B2:B4, Excel says, "Sum the three cells above this one." When you copy the formula to C5, Excel still says to itself, "Sum the three cells above this one" (C2:C4). You don't have to change the formula.

Sometimes you want the reference to stay the same. In this case you use an *absolute reference*. An absolute reference tells Excel to use the named cell; absolutely and positively accept no substitutes! For instance, if you have an interest rate in cell A1, and you have several formulas that refer to that interest rate, you'd use an absolute reference.

TIP

To make a reference absolute, type a dollar sign before the row and column indicators, such as $A$1. To edit a formula and change a reference, press F2. Click the insertion point within the reference; then press F4. Edit the formula, and press Enter to accept the change.

BUZZWORDS

RELATIVE & ABSOLUTE REFERENCES

When you copy or move a formula, relative references change in relation to where they're placed. Absolute references do not change; they always refer to specific cells.

Filling Data

(Letting Excel do the work)

The Fill Down and Fill Right commands on the Edit menu offer a simpler way of copying worksheet formulas. Actually, you can also use this

method to copy words and numbers, but let's focus on formulas for the moment.

To copy a formula down a column of cells, highlight a cell range so that the first cell in the range contains the formula you want to copy and the remaining cells are the blank cells where you'd like to place the copies. Open the Edit menu and choose the Fill Down command, or simply press Ctrl+D, the shortcut key for the Fill Down command. Excel immediately fills in the range with copies of your formula.

To copy a formula across a row of cells, do the same thing, but choose the Fill Right command or press Ctrl+R.

More great ways to fill a cell range with words, numbers, and formulas

▼ You can also copy a formula to the left or up by choosing Fill Left or Fill Up from the Edit menu. Ctrl+H is the shortcut key for the Fill Left command, and Ctrl+W is the shortcut key for Fill Up.

▼ To fill a range with an incremental series of words, move to the cell that contains the first entry, drag the fill handle to select the target range, and then release the mouse. If the first cell contains the word *Jan*, for instance, Excel fills the other cells with *Feb*, *Mar*, *Apr*, and so on.

▼ To fill a range with an incremental series of numbers, type the first two values into two cells that are next to each other. Select the two cells; then drag the fill handle through the range. For instance, to enter the series (10, 20, 30, 40,…), type **10** in one cell and **20** in the next. Then select both cells and drag the fill handle. Excel fills in the rest of the range for you.

BUZZWORDS

FILL HANDLE

Not to be confused with Excel's love handles, the fill handle is the tiny square box that sits in the bottom right corner of the active cell. When you position your mouse pointer on top of a cell's fill handle, the pointer changes from a thick, white cross to a thin, black cross. Drag away, as they say.

This worksheet shows some of the kinds of series you can fill

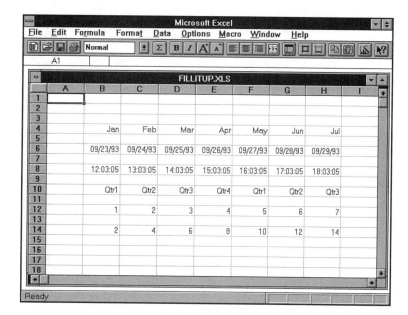

Cool Pasting Techniques

(Going way beyond the call of duty)

Whenever you paste a copy of something into your worksheets, Excel makes an exact duplicate for you. (Except in the case of formulas, as you

saw earlier.) Not only do you get a duplicate of the cell contents, you also get the cell's formatting. The Edit menu contains another pasting command: Paste Special. This command lets *you* decide exactly which parts of your cell range Excel copies. With Paste Special you can achieve copy effects that range from mildly interesting to truly amazing.

Suppose that you spend lots of time typing numbers into a summary section at the top of a worksheet. The numbers you type are actually formula answers from all around the same worksheet. You've tried copying the formula cells directly into the summary section, but their answers keep changing. (All that stuff about relatives, absolutes, and references was too confusing to remember.) Using the Paste Special command, you can quickly copy each formula's answer into the summary section and leave the formula behind.

To use the Paste Special command, select the range you want to copy. Open the Edit menu and choose the Copy command. Select the spot where you want to paste the copied cells, open the Edit menu, and then choose the Paste Special command. Select the option you want; then click OK. You can use only one Paste option at a time with the Paste Special command.

Checklist

▼ The All option copies everything from the target cells into the destination cells. But if your goal is to paste everything, you don't want to do it by using the Paste Special command. Just open the Edit menu and choose Paste; it's much quicker.

▼ The Values option copies only the numbers and words in your cells. Excel converts all formulas to their answers, and displays these numbers in the copied cell range. For example, maybe you want to create a second table of data that summarizes the totals

from a first table. But these displayed totals come from formulas, and you don't necessarily want the formulas in the second table. Use this option to paste them as values instead of formulas.

▼ The Formats option copies only the cell formatting into the copy range. All values and formulas stay behind. This is really helpful after you've formatted a worksheet and realize that you need to use the format from a particular cell elsewhere in the same worksheet. Instead of choosing all the Format commands again, just copy the entire group of formats from one cell to another.

TIP

If your pasting job doesn't go as planned, press Ctrl+Z immediately after using Paste Special to undo the effects on your worksheet.

Switching Rows and Columns

If your worksheet is topsy-turvy with rows that should be columns and columns that should be rows, you can make a quick switch.

Select the range you want to switch. Open the Edit menu and choose the Copy command. Select the spot where you want to put the copied cells. Then open the Edit menu and choose the Paste Special command. Click on the Transpose option to tell Excel to switch the organization of your rows and columns when it pastes the copied cells into the worksheet; then click OK. The following figure shows a "before" and "after" view of how the sample worksheet looks if you use this option.

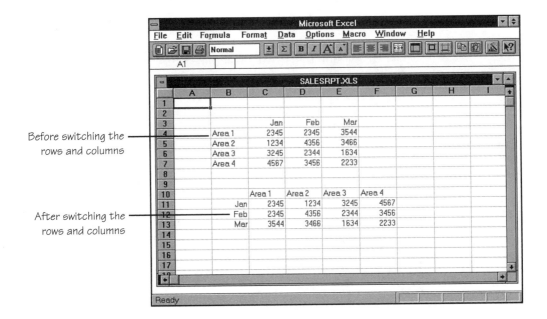

Before switching the rows and columns

After switching the rows and columns

CHAPTER 10

More Worksheet Formatting

(Pretty as a Picture)

IN A NUTSHELL

▼ Creating titles that really
  look centered in a
  worksheet

▼ Adding font effects
  and colors for text

▼ Adding lines and
  borders for clarity

▼ Shading cells to make
  them stand out

▼ Auto-formatting in a
  wink of an eye

E xcel has lots of tools for transforming basic worksheets into stylish, professional-looking documents—the type of documents usually associated with mega-buck marketing departments and Fortune 500 companies.

Earlier you saw how to use a few of these tools to make some formatting changes to your worksheets. You saw how to add bold and italic style to text and how to align words and numbers so that they make sense. (Chapter 5, remember?) Those few tools represent only a small percentage of what's available in Excel's makeup drawer. Now it's time to create even more attractive and innovative looks for your worksheets.

CAUTION

Excel's formatting tools are great fun to use. You can go hog-wild experimenting with all the different combinations (sort of like reassembling Mr. Potato Head a thousand different ways). Keep in mind that when it comes to formatting worksheets, a well-thought plan of attack brings structure, emphasis, and style to your work. Haphazard formatting usually mangles it. If you don't like what you did, you can use the Edit Undo command to undo the change.

What the Heck Is WYSIWYG, Anyway?

(Acronym of the rich and famous)

Great question. WYSIWYG (pronounced "whizzy-wig") is one of the most widely quoted computer terms today. This word actually is an acronym for "what you see is what you get."

The term WYSIWYG came into existence a few years back, when some programs had you formatting your work without actually showing the formatting on-screen. I'm not kidding. Can you imagine a hair stylist cutting your hair while wearing a blindfold? Maybe that's what happened to Sinead O'Connor.

Then along came a whole new class of computer programs that touted themselves as being WYSIWYG products. In other words, what you do on-screen with these programs is exactly (more or less) what you get when you print onto paper. With WYSIWYG programs, you can easily try different formatting effects, see whether you like the effects, and then tinker some more—all before printing.

Selecting the Makeover Candidate

When you format a cell, you start by selecting the cell or cell range you want to format. Chapter 2 covers all the methods for selecting cells.

TIP

Keep in mind that you can select ranges that aren't next to each other. For instance, you might want to change the font in rows 10, 14, 16, and 18. Instead of formatting one row at a time, why not change the font for all four rows at once? Select the first cell range you want to format. Next, hold down the Ctrl key and select the second cell range. Keep holding down the Ctrl key as you select any additional cell ranges. Now format your data. Excel applies your formatting choices to each and every cell you selected.

TIP

For any of the formatting changes you learn in this chapter, you can use the shortcut menu. After you select the cell or range you want to format, click the right mouse button anywhere in the selected range. Excel displays the shortcut menu, from which you choose the command you want.

Parallel Parking and Other Popular Alignments

The easiest way to change the alignment of the data in your worksheet is to select the cells you want to change and use one of the alignment tools on the toolbar, as you learned in Chapter 5. But you have some other options. The three options that are the most fun are centering rows across columns, justifying text, and turning cells topsy-turvy.

To change the alignment of data in a worksheet, select the cell or cell range, open the Format menu, and choose the Alignment command. Excel displays the Alignment dialog box.

The Alignment dialog box shows a complete list of alignment settings for your worksheet data

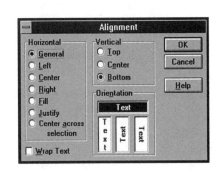

The alignment settings you are most likely to use are discussed next. If you want to experiment, try some of the other choices to see what happens.

Centering Titles

The Center Across Selection alignment option lets you center text or numbers inside the entire width of a selected range of cells. This alignment option makes it easy to center a report title along the top of the worksheet, without having to move it from cell to cell until it looks just right.

Suppose that you typed a report title into cell C2. Then you entered a table of data that uses columns C, D, E, F, and G. The report title in C2 is short. Although it starts in column C, it only extends over into column D. To center the title over the entire table of data (columns C through G), you'd usually have to move it from cell to cell on row 2 until it looks centered. Many times this method doesn't even really center the title; it just gets the title close enough to call it centered.

To *really* center a title across the top of your worksheet, select the range of cells over which you want the title centered. In this case, you'd select cells C2 through G2. (Excel assumes that the title is in the leftmost cell of the range you select. You will get peculiar results if it's not.) Open the Format menu and choose the Alignment command. From the Alignment dialog box, pick the Center Across Selection option and click OK.

Excel centers your title exactly over the range of cells you picked. But here's the wild part: your title stays in its original cell. Excel doesn't move the title anywhere, it just *displays* it in the center of the range you selected. (Don't look for hidden mirrors; there aren't any!)

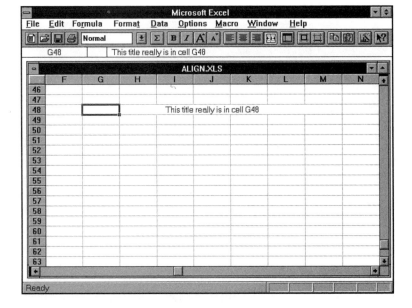

A title centered
across columns
G through M

To quickly center data in a worksheet, select the cell range across which you want the data centered, and then click on the Center Across Columns tool. It's the tool directly to the right of the Right Align tool in the toolbar.

It's a Wrap!

The Wrap Text alignment option is useful for counterattacking the text spillover problem. You know, the problem where you type lots of words into a single cell and they spill into the cell to the right.

If you click on the Wrap Text check box in the Alignment dialog box (so that an X appears in the box), Excel rearranges the words so that they fit the width of the current cell. No, Excel doesn't lop off anything. It just elongates the cell from top to bottom and shuffles the words onto several lines so that everything fits. In other words, Excel increases the row height setting for that cell's row.

Microsoft Excel							
File	Edit	Formula	Format	Data	Options	Macro	Window	Help

C13   This text is wrapped because it's too long to fit into the width of this column.

ALIGN.XLS

	A	B	C	D	E	F	G
10							
11							
12							
13			This text is wrapped because it's too long to fit into the width of this column.				
14							
15							
16							
17							
18							
19							
20							
21							
22							
23							
24							
25							

Ready

Wrapping text in a worksheet cell

Stacked and Sideways Text

For a cool special effect, you can spin text so that it sits on its side. Open the Format menu and choose the Alignment command. Take a look at the area labeled Orientation in the Alignment dialog box. The four boxes with the word *Text* show the different choices. To use a different orientation for your data, click on the box you want.

Here are some
rotated row
headings

Fonts Are Our Friends

With Excel, you can easily change the look of numbers and text in
your worksheets. A good way to grab someone's attention with your
worksheet is to change the characteristics of its type—the font, the
size, the style, or the color.

BUZZWORDS

FONT

A font is a set of characters (like A–Z or 1–9) in a particular
typeface, such as Helvetica or Times Roman.

To enhance the appearance of your data, select the cell or cell range you
want to change, open the Format menu, and choose the Font command.

Excel displays the Font dialog box. From this box, you can choose a new font, pick a style, choose a different size, and more! The next sections tell you how to do all this stuff.

The options in the Font dialog box determine how words and numbers look in your worksheet

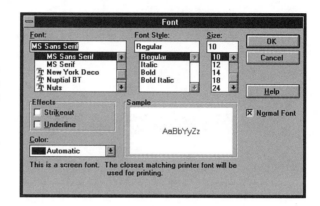

After you're finished making changes in the Font dialog box, click OK to return to your worksheet. Excel (being the WYSIWYG wizard that it is) immediately puts your font choices into effect.

Fonts Have Feelings, Too

Different fonts say different things. Some look conservative and businesslike; others feel fun and fanciful. The fonts you choose for your worksheets should convey the right impression to the reader. You can change both the font and the font size.

Goudy	**Revue**
Helvetica	𝕱𝖊𝖙𝖙𝖊 𝕱𝖗𝖆𝖐𝖙𝖚𝖗
Hobo	Tekton

The Font box contains a list of all the fonts you can use in your worksheet. Click on the up or down scroll arrows to check out what's available on your list. Then click on the font you want.

The Size box contains a list of the point sizes that are available for the current font. Click on the up or down scroll arrows to see all the available sizes. For most fonts, you can choose sizes from 1 point to 72 points. Click on the size you want.

BUZZWORDS

POINT SIZE

Fonts are measured in point sizes from 1 point to 72. There's about 72 points per inch.

TIP

Unless you're one of those lucky folks who spent lots of money buying extra fonts, your font choices are limited to the ones that come with the Microsoft Windows package.

When a report needs that extra special something, but you just don't have the right fonts for the job, here's what to do: ask your favorite computer nerd to help you purchase additional fonts for your computer. Heck, convince him or her to pay for the fonts. But be sure to pick someone who has both an opinion about different brands of fonts and the desire and time to help you install them. (Keep in mind that the fonts you choose must work with your particular printer.)

BUZZWORDS

TRUETYPE FONTS

Here's another buzzword for the next office party: "TrueType fonts" (as if you'd buy something called FalseType fonts). These kinds of fonts are the current rage if you're running Windows and Excel on your computer. That's because TrueType fonts are versatile (they come in virtually every size you could possibly need), inexpensive (I've seen packages of 100 fonts that sell for about $40), and come in about a billion different flavors (from Astaire to Zorba.) The next time you're asked which class of fonts you prefer, just say "Why, TrueType, of course."

Stylizing a Font

In addition to picking the font and the size, you can change the font style. Add bold and italic formatting to your worksheet data to make titles and row headings stand out. These font styles help a reader scan a worksheet quickly and find important data—that is, the data *you* think is important. After all, you're the one who's doing the formatting.

TIP

Remember, you can quickly apply a bold or italic style to your data by selecting the cells you want to format and then clicking on the Bold or Italic tool on the toolbar.

Special Font FX

In the Effects area of the Font dialog box, you can choose Strikeout and Underline. The following sample worksheet shows what these effects look like. You decide for yourself whether they're worthwhile. (In an upcoming section, you'll learn a better way to draw lines under cells.)

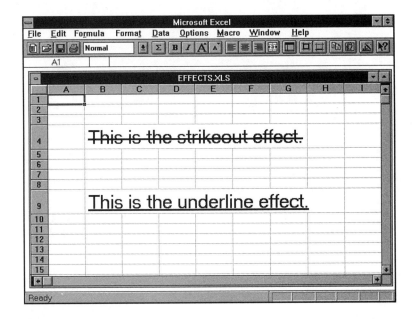

Special effects you can create by using the Fonts dialog box

Color Me Blue (Or yellow, or red, or...)

Color can create feelings and convey impressions in ways that simply can't be achieved with other formatting tools. I'm green with envy. The firm's in the black. You're singing the blues. Have fun with color in your Excel worksheets. But remember that too much color can blind your reader, and certain color combinations are guaranteed to cause migraine headaches.

The Font dialog box has a Color list that shows all the different colors you can use for the text in your worksheets. To activate this list, click on the down arrow at the right edge of the list box. Then click on the color you want. Keep in mind that unless you have a color printer, the colors won't print. You're stuck with black and white.

Headin' for the Borders

After you've made basic formatting changes to your worksheet, you might want to add a few finishing touches. Borders are one effective way to highlight important worksheet data. A border can be a single line drawn on one side of a cell, such as the top or left side, or lines surrounding a cell. It's up to you.

TIP

Removing the gridlines from around your worksheet cells improves the view of many worksheet formatting effects, particularly borders and shading (that's next). To remove gridlines, open the Options menu and choose the Display command. In the Display dialog box, uncheck the Gridlines option by clicking on it, and then click OK to return to your worksheet. The gridlines disappear.

To add borders to a cell range, select the range, open the Format menu, and choose the Border command. Your options are Outline (all sides), Left, Right, Top, and Bottom. Next, choose the style of line you want to use. Your line style options, clockwise from the upper left corner of the Style block, are the following: Hairline, Thin, Medium, Thick, Double, Dotted, Dashed, and None.

The borders aren't turning out the way I want!

In an Excel worksheet, cells that sit side-by-side always share borders. For example, the right edge of cell D4 is also the left edge of cell E4, and the top of cell H6 is also the bottom of cell H5. When you add a border to a cell, keep in mind that you're also adding it to the adjacent cell. You might have to tinker around with the borders to get them just the way you want.

When you choose a line style, a sample of the line style appears to the left of the border position you selected in the Border block. You can use any combination of positions and line styles for the cell or cell range you select. For example, if you select a position and style for the top of the cell, you can select a different line style for the bottom or sides of the cell.

Borders help set apart different groups of data in a worksheet

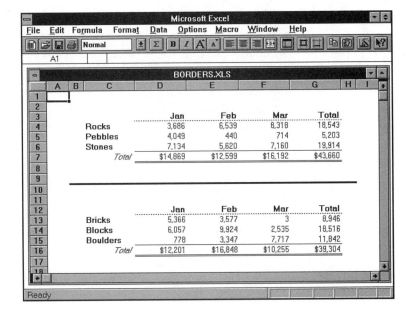

To quickly apply outline and bottom borders to data in a worksheet, select the data and then click on the Outline Border tool or Bottom Border tool in the toolbar. They're the two tools to the left of the Copy tool in the toolbar.

Restin' Under a Shady Cell

Another way to call attention to important stuff in your worksheet is to "shade" the cells. To do so, select the cell range you want to shade, open the Format menu, and choose the Patterns command. Excel displays the Patterns dialog box. You can shade your selected cells with a solid color, a pattern, or a combination of both.

To choose a pattern, click on the down arrow next to the Patterns style box. Choose a pattern from the Pattern list that Excel displays. To choose a color, click on the down arrow next to the Foreground style box. Excel displays a list of colors. Choose a color, and then click OK.

If you choose a pattern, the color you pick from the Foreground list will be applied to the pattern, not to the cell's background; for example, if you choose a dotted pattern, the dots will appear in whatever color you pick from the Foreground list. To change the color that's behind the pattern, click on the down arrow next to the Background style box in the Patterns dialog box, and choose a color.

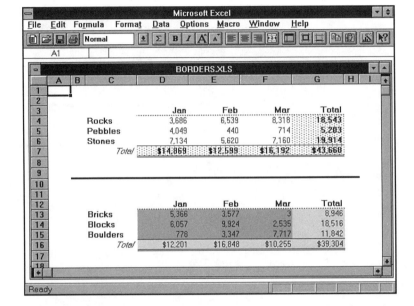

A few cell-shading effects you can create with a little practice

Checklist

▼ When you create shades for your worksheet cells, use light colors so that you don't obscure the contents of a cell.

▼ To return to the standard window foreground and background colors, scroll to the bottom of their respective lists and choose Automatic.

▼ To use no pattern whatsoever, open the Patterns list box, scroll down to the None option, and then click OK.

▼ You can also apply shading from the Borders dialog box by clicking on the Shading check box, but the shading looks nicer if you use the Patterns command instead.

Auto-Formatting Tables of Data

When the expiration date on your creative juices has long since expired, Excel proudly presents you with the AutoFormat command. This feature takes all the hassle of making formatting decisions for tables and places it firmly on the shoulders of Excel. All you have to do is choose from several predefined format styles.

CAUTION

This feature works only on tables—data set up in rows and columns, with row and column headings. If your data is not set up as a table, you'll have to do the formatting by hand.

Select the entire table of data, open the Format menu, and choose the AutoFormat command. Excel displays the AutoFormat dialog box, in which you choose a table format from a list of 14 pre-designed formats. Just pick the one you want! The Sample box in the middle of the AutoFormat dialog box shows you how the table will look with that format. If you like it, click OK.

In this example, the Sample box shows you what the table format called "Colorful 2" will look like

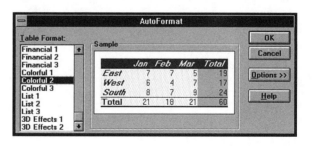

To quickly apply the default table format—or to apply the last one you used, if you've used this feature before and changed the default—select another table of data in your worksheet and click on the AutoFormat tool in the toolbar. This tool is situated to the right of the Center Across Columns tool.

CHAPTER 11

Beyond Basic Printing

IN A NUTSHELL

▼ Other ways to start a printer printing

▼ Printing more than one copy, and other fun stuff

▼ Being selective about what to print

▼ Adding print titles for big worksheets

▼ Controlling the look of the printout

▼ Adding headers and footers

▼ Using the Print Manager to speed things up

Excel gives you total control over printing. Now, that may or may not be a good thing. Most folks are comfortable knowing only the bare-bones essentials of printing (like what's covered in Chapter 6). Some people want to understand these same essentials plus a few other features, like how to print parts of a worksheet, change margins, and switch between draft-quality and letter-quality printing. The remaining three people are the ones who absolutely have to know every single nuance of printing in Excel, from printing sideways on a three-part carbon to printing worksheets in Swahili to disassembling and reassembling a printer in 40 seconds flat while blindfolded.

This chapter is for the middle group of people. If you are in this group, you might want to know how to print a range of selected worksheet cells. Or how to print more than one copy of a worksheet without having to sit at your desk and choose the Print command over and over again. Or maybe you just want to know how to add a date and page number to the bottom of your printouts.

If you're not in this group, skip this chapter. (But you just might miss something....)

Basic Printing Revisited

(For just a second or two)

Chapter 6 shows you how easy it is to print in Excel. With a worksheet on-screen, you simply open the File menu and choose the Print command; then click OK inside the Print dialog box. Printing this way requires no special preparation or advanced degrees. Here are some other ways to print an Excel worksheet.

▼ Click on the Print tool. It's the icon fourth from the left in the toolbar and looks like a little printer. This prints everything in the current worksheet.

▼ Press Ctrl+Shift+F12, the shortcut key for the Print command. This displays the Print dialog box. Click OK or press Enter to begin printing everything in the current worksheet.

TIP

It's always a good idea to save a worksheet before printing it. That way you won't lose any information if your computer suddenly dies on you, or if you accidentally flip off the power switch or hit the Reset button while Excel is printing.

Printing More Than One Copy, and Other Fun Stuff

When you want to exert just a little bit more control over your print-outs, open the Print dialog box and select one of these options:

▼ If you want to print a draft of your worksheet, click on the down arrow next to Print Quality. The list that appears shows you the different qualities your printer can achieve. Printing quality is measured in terms of *dots per inch* (dpi). The more dots, the higher the quality and more professional-looking your printouts will be. The less dots, the quicker the worksheet will print.

continues

▼ To print more than one copy of your worksheet, highlight the Copies box and type the number of copies you want to print.

▼ For a quick printout without graphics, click on "The Fast, but no graphics" check box.

Controlling What Excel Prints

When you print a worksheet, Excel prints the whole darn thing unless you tell it otherwise. That's fine when your worksheet is fairly small. But if the worksheet is 200 columns wide and 5,000 rows long, it'd take you a full workday just to churn out that baby. More often than not, you'll be selective when it comes to what stuff gets printed from your worksheet.

Printing a Range of Pages

If you want to print just certain pages, open the Print dialog box. Click on the Pages option. In the From box, enter the starting page number. In the To box, enter the ending page number. Then click OK. Excel will print the selected pages.

"I HATE THIS!"

What equals a page?

Margins, column width, and other things affect what will print on one page.

To figure out where Excel is going to split the pages when you print your worksheet, use the Print Preview command (it's on the File menu).

Printing a Particular Area of Your Worksheet

If you want to print just a particular area of your worksheet, start by selecting the range of cells you want to print. Next, open the Options menu and choose the Set Print Area command. This command draws a dotted line around the cell range you selected so that Excel knows exactly what to print. Next, open the File menu and choose the Print command; then click OK to begin printing.

Here's how to be really selective about the information you print. In your worksheet, select several different cell ranges that are not connected. (Remember to hold down Ctrl while you select each disconnected range.) Next, open the Options menu and choose the Set Print Area command. Notice that Excel does not display the dotted lines around your disconnected cell ranges. Don't worry, it's supposed to be that way. Finally, print the worksheet. When you print a group of disconnected cell ranges, Excel prints each selection on its own page.

TIP

Check out your worksheet in a Print Preview window before you print it. That way you'll be sure that you've selected the correct cell ranges.

"I HATE THIS!"

I changed my mind. I want to print the whole thing!

If you print part of a worksheet and then want to print the entire worksheet, you've got to tell Excel about the change; otherwise, it looks for the selected print area because the Set Print Area command is still on. Select the entire worksheet (click in the small area above the row numbers and to the left of the column letters). Then open the Options menu and choose the Remove Print Area command. This resets the print range.

Bestowing Titles upon Your Worksheet

A print title is text that Excel prints at the top and/or left side of each page in a printout. Print titles are the row and column headings, and they're great for worksheets that just don't seem to fit on a single printed page. Consider the worksheet on the opposite page. It's so wide that everything beyond column H has to be printed on another page. The problem is that the second page doesn't show what the rows mean. (A potential disaster if these two pages accidentally get separated at birth.)

To solve this problem, add some print titles:

1. Select the worksheet area you want to print, open the Options menu, and choose the Set Print Area command.

2. Open the Options menu and choose the Set Print Titles command.

3. In the Set Print Titles dialog box, click inside the Titles for Rows text box. (You want to create row titles for the second page in the printout.)

4. Click on the column in your worksheet that contains the row titles you want to display on all pages of the printout. You can select several columns for titles by dragging across the columns you want.

For the sample worksheet, you'd click on column A. Excel displays a marquee around the entire column you select. The column letter now appears in the Titles for Rows box.

5. Click OK to return to the worksheet.

6. Print your worksheet.

	A	B	C	D	E	F	G	H
1								
2								
3		Jan	Feb	Mar	Apr	May	Jun	Jul
4	Rent	10,000	10,000	10,000	10,000	10,000	10,000	10,000
5	Telephone	6,401	5,278	4,217	6,734	4,632	5,050	387
6	Utilities	8,067	519	1,154	6,793	8,372	584	9,688
7	Insurance	4,482	5,654	8,232	2,527	6,454	9,804	9,952
8	Contract Labor	6,298	1,400	2,551	9,648	4,219	9,457	748
9	Commissions	8,955	2,723	7,298	6,078	2,004	3,723	6,008
10	Accounting	3,110	4,967	1,455	6,539	8,751	2,979	6,318
11	Legal	5,924	4,324	5,485	9,648	7,760	2,535	2,885
12	Furniture	5,525	1,121	947	7,501	9,966	3,538	1,414
13	Hardware	5,570	5,286	4,583	9,831	7,505	5,867	6,138
14	Software	7,123	8,787	7,736	3,529	1,371	1,432	2,231
15	Postage	526	6,174	8,057	3,972	9,670	9,177	4,187
16	TOTAL	$71,981	$56,233	$61,715	$82,800	$80,704	$64,146	$59,956
17								

Excel printed
this worksheet
on two pages
because it's too
wide to fit on one

	I	J	K	L	M
1					
2					
3	Aug	Sep	Oct	Nov	Dec
4	10,000	10,000	10,000	10,000	10,000
5	7,366	7,035	2,878	2,277	9,383
6	6,834	350	3,034	8,857	5,879
7	5,082	5,755	734	4,102	5,757
8	3,531	8,910	6,303	5,399	2,361
9	581	9,864	5,523	9,082	1,881
10	1,771	9,518	719	8,672	4,123
11	3,294	3,905	558	3,809	5,314
12	7,386	4,643	690	490	2,102
13	2,648	3,661	1,889	1,273	8,426
14	6,239	2,153	9,471	6,597	9,246
15	9,988	16	9,173	2,626	3,027
16	$64,720	$65,810	$50,972	$63,184	$67,499
17					

Here's what the printout of the sample worksheet looks like now that the row headings from column A have been repeated on the second page in the worksheet.

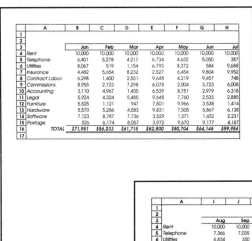

	A	B	C	D	E	F	G	H
1								
2								
3		Jan	Feb	Mar	Apr	May	Jun	Jul
4	Rent	10,000	10,000	10,000	10,000	10,000	10,000	10,000
5	Telephone	6,401	5,278	4,217	6,734	4,632	5,050	387
6	Utilities	8,067	519	1,154	6,793	8,372	584	9,688
7	Insurance	4,482	5,654	8,232	2,527	6,454	9,804	9,952
8	Contract Labor	6,298	1,400	2,551	9,648	4,219	9,457	748
9	Commissions	8,955	2,723	7,298	6,078	2,004	3,723	6,008
10	Accounting	3,110	4,967	1,455	6,539	8,751	2,979	6,318
11	Legal	5,924	4,324	5,485	9,548	7,760	2,535	2,885
12	Furniture	5,525	1,121	947	7,501	9,966	3,538	1,414
13	Hardware	5,570	5,286	4,583	9,831	7,505	5,867	6,138
14	Software	7,123	8,787	7,736	3,529	1,371	1,432	2,231
15	Postage	526	6,174	8,057	3,972	9,670	9,177	4,187
16	TOTAL	$71,981	$56,233	$61,715	$82,800	$80,704	$64,146	$59,956
17								

Now it's easy to see what the rows mean on the second page of the printout

	A	I	J	K	L	M
1						
2						
3		Aug	Sep	Oct	Nov	Dec
4	Rent	10,000	10,000	10,000	10,000	10,000
5	Telephone	7,366	7,035	2,878	2,277	9,383
6	Utilities	6,834	350	3,034	8,857	5,879
7	Insurance	5,082	5,755	734	4,102	5,757
8	Contract Labor	3,531	8,910	6,303	5,399	2,361
9	Commissions	581	9,864	5,523	9,082	1,881
10	Accounting	1,771	9,518	719	8,672	4,123
11	Legal	3,294	3,905	558	3,809	5,314
12	Furniture	7,386	4,643	690	490	2,102
13	Hardware	2,648	3,661	1,889	1,273	8,426
14	Software	6,239	2,153	9,471	6,597	9,246
15	Postage	9,988	16	9,173	2,626	3,027
16	TOTAL	$64,720	$65,810	$50,972	$63,184	$67,499
17						

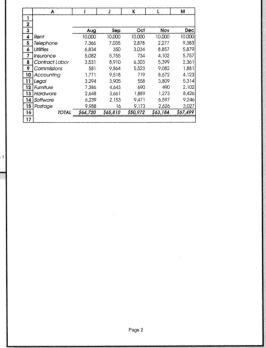

Page 1

Page 2

▼ You also can print titles by using text from the top of a worksheet. This is great for narrow worksheets that have tons of rows of information. For that situation, click inside the Titles for Columns text box in the Set Print Titles dialog box, and then click on the row that contains the titles you want displayed at the top of each printed page. For example, you might click on row 3 in the sample worksheet to display the month headings at the top of each page in the printout. You also can drag across multiple rows to get several rows of titles.

▼ To cancel any worksheet titles you've created, simply reopen the Set Print Titles dialog box and delete the information from the appropriate box.

Adding Page Breaks

Excel automatically decides where to split the pages of your worksheet when you print it; however, Excel also allows you to add *page breaks* to your worksheet. A page break tells Excel where to start a new page during printing. To force a page break, select the row above which you want a page break. Then open the File menu and choose the Set Page Break command.

Tinkering with Printing Special Effects

In Excel, the phrase "page setup" is used to describe all the changeable things about the pages in your printouts. It's not the information

contained in the worksheet itself, but the way stuff is laid out on the printed page. Like whether the worksheet prints up and down a page or across a page or whether the row letters and column numbers and gridlines are printed. And other stuff.

For most worksheets, you'll be happy to use Excel's normal settings. When you want to change these settings for one of your Excel worksheets (you masochist, you), open the File menu and choose the Page Setup command. Welcome to the world of desktop publishing for spreadsheets, where the decisions to be made seem endless.

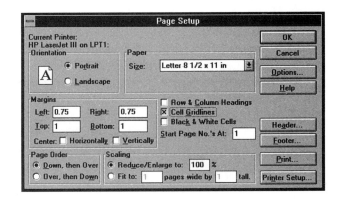

Reviewing the options in the Page Setup dialog box

TIP

There are two other ways to get to the Page Setup dialog box: click on the Page Setup option in the Print dialog box, or click on the Setup button in the Print Preview window.

Checklist

▼ The Orientation options tell Excel which direction to print: the Portrait option is the usual way to print, and the Landscape option prints everything sideways on the paper.

▼ The Paper option tells Excel what size paper you're using. The normal setting for this option is Letter 8 1/2 × 11. That's the size of a typical piece of printer paper. To use a different size (such as legal size), click on the down arrow next to the Size option. Then click on the size you want. Keep in mind that your printer has to be able to handle these different sizes of paper. You can't jam legal-sized paper into the regular printer tray and hope that everything prints okay.

▼ The Margins settings control how many inches of blank space appear between the outside edge of the paper and the printed information. Rather than mess around with typing settings, you can use the Center Horizontally and Center Vertically check boxes to center the printed information on the paper, regardless of any margin settings you've selected.

▼ The Row & Column Headings check box determines whether row numbers and column letters appear as part of your printout. Normally they don't, so this box is unchecked. Check it if you want to show them.

▼ The Cell Gridlines check box determines whether the lines that appear around your cells also show up on your printout. Normally they do, so this box is checked. To print without showing them, check the box.

▼ The Black & White Cells check box tells Excel to ignore the colors you've added to your worksheet and print it using only black and white. This box is normally unchecked. Check it when cells in your printout look faded or are difficult to read.

▼ The Start Page No.'s At option tells Excel which page number to print on the first page of your worksheet. Normally this is set to 1, but if you want to start numbering with a different number, type that number in the entry blank.

continues

▼ The Scaling options allow you to change the size of information in your printouts. Choose the Fit option to automatically scale a worksheet (or a selected range of cells) to fit onto a single printed page. The normal settings are 1 page wide by 1 page tall, which tells Excel to fit your data onto a single printed page. Type other numbers to fit your data into more or less space, as desired. To cram a large block of worksheet data onto a single page, click on the Reduce/Enlarge button and type a percent number between 10 and 400 in the box. Anything under 100% shrinks the worksheet data, and anything over 100% enlarges the data in the printout.

Changing the Headers and Footers

Headers and footers are extra text you can include at the top and bottom, respectively, of each page in a printout. A header appears at the top, and a footer at the bottom.

Excel normally shows the worksheet file name at the top and the page number at the bottom of your worksheet printouts. To change a header or footer, open the Page Setup dialog box and click on the Header or Footer button. Excel displays the Header or Footer dialog box, depending on which button you choose (both dialog boxes look exactly the same, except for the title).

Note that Excel uses a special code for the file name and page number (take a look at the next Experts Only box). If you want to change the text to something different, select the text and type something new. Anything you type in the Left Section window appears at the left edge of the printout; anything in the Center Section window appears in the

center; and (you guessed it) anything in the Right Section window appears at the right edge of the printout.

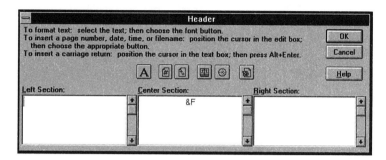

The Header dialog box contains three section windows into which you can type text

EXPERTS ONLY

Secret codes for headers and footers

Look at the preceding figure closely. Notice that strange-looking thing in the middle section? That &F thing is the code for file name. The code for page number is &P. The easiest way to include one these codes in header or footer text is to click in the window section where you want to show the information and then click one of the special code buttons. Here's what these buttons do:

 Displays the font dialog box so that you can change fonts for your text

 Inserts the current page number code

 Inserts the code for the total number of pages in a printout

 Inserts the current date code

EXPERTS ONLY

 Inserts the current time code

 Inserts the file name code

For clarity, you also can type text before or after one of these codes. For instance, if you type **Page**, press the space bar once, and click on the # tool, the footer on the fifth page would look like this: Page 5.

To show where this page is in relation to all the pages in the printout, type this entry: **Page &P of &N**. On the seventh page of a ten-page printout, this is how the footer would look: Page 7 of 10.

Help! I Can't Seem To Manage Printing in Excel

Printing can be the most time-consuming aspect of working with computer software. Have you ever had to sit around and wait for your printer to finish printing before you could continue working with Excel? Printing speeds can be different from computer to computer. Some computers can print Excel worksheets in the blink of an eye. Others seem to blink a few times, blink a few more, and then blink even more before they start printing a worksheet.

When your computer runs more like a Geo than a Porsche, you might be able to soup it up so that your worksheets print faster. To do this, turn on the Windows Print Manager program, as explained in the next section. Once on, the Print Manager takes over responsibility for printing your worksheets, allowing you to keep working in Excel with a minimum

of interruptions. When the Print Manager is off, Excel itself must deal with the printing chores, which means that you'll have to wait anywhere from a few seconds to a half hour before you can continue working in Excel.

Turning On the Print Manager

You activate the Print Manager from the Printers utility in the Control Panel. If that last sentence made absolutely no sense to you, remain calm, take a few deep breaths, and follow these steps:

1. From the Program Manager (the main Windows screen), double-click on the Main group icon to open its window—that is, unless it's already open. Then double-click on the Control Panel program icon.

2. In the Control Panel window, double-click on the Printers icon. Windows displays the Printers dialog box.

The Printers dialog box is where you activate the Print Manager

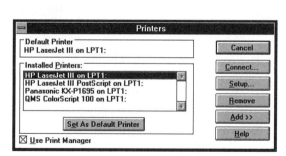

3. Click on the Use Print Manager check box (if it isn't already selected).

Nothing spectacular will happen on your screen after you activate the Print Manager. Just keep printing the same old way you have been. You'll continue to see the same Printing dialog box that appears while you're printing. The only noticeable difference will be that the Printing dialog box disappears much more quickly with the Print Manager on the job! The faster that box goes away, the faster you can get back to your Excel work.

Choosing a Printer

Excel prints to the default printer (the one that's selected) in the Print Manager every time you choose the Print command from the File menu. You're allowed to have only one default printer at a time, so be sure to pick the one you use most often. Here's how to select a new default printer:

1. Open the Printers dialog box, as explained in the preceding steps.

2. In the Installed Printers box, click on the printer you want to use as the default printer.

3. Click on the Set As Default Printer button. Windows displays your printer's name in the Default Printer box at the top of the Printers dialog box.

4. Click on the Close button to close the Printers dialog box. Windows returns you to the Control Panel.

5. Open the Settings menu and choose the Exit command.

You're now done with the Printers program. Windows returns you to the Program Manager.

CHAPTER 12

Excel Does Windows

IN A NUTSHELL

▼ Resizing your worksheet window
▼ Viewing the same worksheet in two different windows
▼ Hiding worksheet windows
▼ Splitting worksheet windows
▼ Freezing window panes
▼ Zooming in and out

xcel's Window menu is the loneliest menu of all. It sits way down at the right end of the menu bar, next to the Help menu. It's easy to forget that there's a Window menu in Excel because, well, when we think of windows, it's usually Microsoft Windows, the graphical program, that comes to mind.

The Window menu is a wallflower because, frankly, its commands just aren't the nuts and bolts of the program. You don't add or subtract with the Window menu commands. You can't print with them either. You can't even insert a row or save your worksheet from this menu.

So what the heck is the Window menu for? This chapter will show you. You'll learn some truly unique ways of looking at your worksheets—ways that make entering and updating data easier.

Controlling Your Worksheet Window

Have you ever noticed that every time you create a new worksheet, its window fills up most—but not all—of your Excel screen? There's always a white or gray area behind the worksheet. You can enlarge a worksheet so that it fills up this space. You also can move it around inside this space. You can accomplish these feats and many other, similar appearance-altering tricks.

"I HATE THIS!"

A window is a window is a window

When you start Excel, the program is displayed in a window—known as the "program window." Each Excel worksheet you create sits in its own window, which somebody at Microsoft once decided should be officially known as a "document window." But that sounds pretty formal, so the rest of us have always called it exactly what it is: a worksheet window. The area behind the worksheet window is called the workspace, or the space in which you do your work in Excel.

The easiest way to work with the window is to use the mouse:

Checklist

▼ To move a worksheet, you just drag its title bar around the workspace.

▼ To resize a worksheet, drag one of its window borders.

▼ To minimize the worksheet (turn it into an icon), click on the Minimize button. Be sure to click on the Minimize button in the worksheet window, not in the Excel window, which also has a Minimize button. To go from the icon back to the worksheet, double-click on the minimized icon.

▼ To maximize the worksheet (zoom it to full-screen), click on the Maximize button. When a worksheet is fully enlarged in the workspace, you can't resize the window, and the Restore button replaces the Minimize and Maximize buttons. Click on the Restore button to return to the original worksheet size.

continues

I HATE EXCEL!

▼ To close a worksheet, double-click on the Control menu icon. You'll be reminded to save your worksheet, if you haven't already.

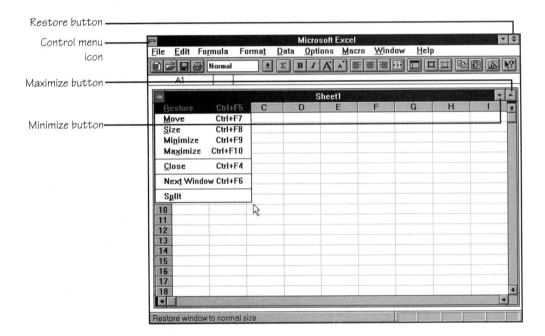

Restore button

Control menu icon

Maximize button

Minimize button

TIP

You can also use the commands on a worksheet's Control menu. (Don't look for the word "Control" in the menu bar; it's not there.) To get to a worksheet's Control menu, click on the Control menu icon once. It's the one that looks like a hyphen in the upper left corner of the worksheet. Don't confuse the worksheet's Control menu icon (a short dash) with Excel's Control menu icon (a long dash). Once the menu is open, choose the command you want.

TIP

Another way to control your windows is by using the keyboard shortcuts for the Control menu commands:

Ctrl+F5	Restore a window
Ctrl+F7, arrow keys	Move a window
Ctrl+F8, arrow keys	Resize a window
Ctrl+F9	Minimize a window
Ctrl+F10	Maximize a window
Ctrl+F4	Close a window
Ctrl+F6	Select the next window

Looking at the Same Worksheet Twice

(Double vision)

Excel allows you to create a copy of the active worksheet and place the copy in its own window. Then you can rearrange both windows on your screen so that you can see different parts of each, just like if you could look through a microscope and see two different parts of the same slide.

There are several good reasons why you want to do something like this. ("Because it's there," isn't one of them. Really.) The truth is, as you work more and more in Excel, you'll become comfortable creating wider and longer worksheets. It's inevitable. Creating a new window for a large worksheet makes it easier to quickly move around and find stuff.

Suppose that you have a really long worksheet open in Excel. The formulas are way down on row 500, but the data you're changing is way up

on row 50. You're updating your payroll budget report, and it's import-ant that you keep an eye on the bottom-line figure as you enter each new number into the worksheet. After all, heads will roll if you go over budget.

Opening a Second Window

First, create a new window by opening the Window menu and choosing the New Window command. Excel opens a second window that overlays the first. It looks almost exactly the same as the first one. The only dif-ference is that at the end of the worksheet name in the title bar, there's a colon followed by a number. That's the window number. Your original window is window 1, and the new window is window 2.

Checklist

▼ Excel lets you create as many windows as your computer's memory can handle. It's easiest when you stick to a maximum of four to five windows. Any more than that, and your screen will feel over-crowded. This makes it difficult to work effectively with the open windows.

▼ You can move back and forth between windows by pointing and clicking inside a window or by pressing Ctrl+F6.

▼ When a worksheet has more than one window, information that you enter into one window also appears in the other.

▼ The names of all open worksheets and worksheet windows appear in the bottom of the Window menu. The one that's currently active will have a check mark next to it. You can choose a name from this list (just as if you were choosing a command) to make that one the active worksheet or window.

▼ If you use the File Save command to save a worksheet you're displaying in two or more windows, only the original worksheet file is saved. Excel does not save any of the other, duplicate worksheets.

Arranging the Windows

Now you'll want to arrange the windows on-screen so that you can see both of them, because chances are that one window covers up part of the other. Ideally, you want them displayed in such a way that it's easy to watch your formula answers change as you type in new numbers. Open the Window menu and choose the Arrange command. When the Arrange Windows dialog box appears, click on the Horizontal button, and then click OK. Here's what your screen should look like:

Two windows arranged horizontally, one on top of the other

	Microsoft Excel							
File **Edit** **Formula** **Format** **Data** **Options** **Macro** **Window** **Help**								

A485

PAYROLL.XLS:1

	A	B	C	D	E	F	G	H
1	Payroll Budget Report							
2	Fiscal 1993							
3								
4		Jan	Feb	Mar	Apr	May	Jun	Jul
5	Bob	1,588	1,724	1,552	1,747	1,647	1,664	1,631
6	Carol	1,729	1,736	1,504	1,522	1,641	1,710	1,683
7	Ted	1,681	1,649	1,559	1,740	1,582	1,588	1,566
8	Alice	1,609	1,653	1,658	1,681	1,706	1,710	1,647

PAYROLL.XLS:2

	A	B	C	D	E	F	G	H
494	Carl	3,162	3,043	3,162	3,247	3,147	3,180	3,090
495	Matt	3,009	3,237	3,001	3,020	3,161	3,247	3,185
496	Sue	3,179	3,063	3,229	3,089	3,183	3,242	3,098
497	Trevor	3,157	3,107	3,186	3,070	3,228	3,149	3,168
498	Phyllis	3,015	3,219	3,006	3,099	3,106	3,195	3,109
499	TOTAL	$45,041	$45,096	$44,938	$45,873	$45,598	$45,869	$45,863
500								
501								

Ready

A horizontal window arrangement is ideal for this worksheet. That's because this worksheet has lots and lots of information on rows. (It's only 14 columns wide.) Other worksheet layouts might require a different arrangement of windows. Here's what the other window-arranging options do:

▼ The Tiled option lays out all windows in a tile fashion.

▼ The Vertical option arranges windows in a side-by-side fashion. This layout is useful when your worksheets have lots of columns of information.

▼ Use the None option in combination with the Sync options (explained next) when you want to make all open windows scroll together, without arranging them on-screen at the same time.

▼ The Windows of Active Document options let you synchronize your windows. This means, for example, that when you scroll one column to the right in a window, all other open windows also scroll one column to the right. For this feature to work, you must click on the Sync Horizontal and/or Sync Vertical check boxes in the Arrange Windows dialog box.

▼ When you synchronize windows to scroll together, Excel displays a code on each window's title bar, next to the file name. This is how you know when synchronization has been set for the windows. The [HSync] code means that you've set the windows to scroll horizontally; the [VSync] code means they're set to scroll vertically; and the [HVSync] code means they'll scroll both horizontally and vertically.

▼ For a different angle on how to arrange two windows, see the upcoming section "Splitting a Window into Two."

To close a window after you're finished working with it, make the window active, open its Control menu, and choose the Close command. Keyboarders can simply press Ctrl+F4. When there's only one open window left on your screen, you're back to the original window.

TIP

When you create several windows for a worksheet, each one looks exactly the same as the next window. You can create unique display views for different windows. For instance, you might want to remove the display of cell gridlines from one window but not the other. To accomplish these display effects, click on the window you want to change, and then choose the Display command from the Options menu. See Chapter 18 for more information about changing the display settings for a worksheet.

Working on Two Files at Once (Double duty)

Some of the more adventurous Excel users enjoy working with more than one worksheet at a time. This is easy enough to accomplish; you just use the File Open command to open as many as you'd like. With two different worksheets open, you can see key figures in one worksheet, and copy data from one to the other.

Checklist

▼ When you have several worksheets open at once, but the active worksheet isn't the one you want to work in, you can select the one you want. Open the Window menu. All open worksheets are listed at the bottom of the menu. Click on the name of the one you want. A quicker method is to click on the open worksheet, if you can see it.

continues

CHAPTER 12

Checklist, continued

▼ To arrange all the worksheets you are working on, go back and read the section before this one, "Arranging the Windows."

▼ To close a worksheet, save it and then either double-click on the Control menu icon for that window or open the File menu and choose the Close command.

TIP

Because this several-files-open-at-once tactic has a tendency to fill up the workspace, you might want to try this trick: minimize all worksheets you're not using at the moment, so that they're displayed as icons at the bottom of the workspace. To do this, open the Control menu and choose the Minimize command. Whenever your icons get messy in the workspace, open the Window menu and choose the Arrange Icons command. Yes, I know that it wasn't on your Window menu when you looked before. In fact, the only time the Arrange Icons command does appear on the Window menu is when (…drum roll please…) you've minimized a worksheet to the size of an icon and that icon is active.

Splitting a Window into Two

(Panes, that is)

The Split command works a lot like the Arrange command. You use it to check out two distant parts of the same worksheet. The difference is that you don't create a second window when you use the Split command. You actually create two panes in the same worksheet window.

Here's how: Position the active cell in the area of the worksheet where you'd like the split to occur. To create two horizontal panes, for example, you might position the active cell in row A9. To create two vertical panes, position the active cell in column E1. Now open the Window menu and choose the Split command. As soon as you choose Split, Excel divides the worksheet into two panes.

Creating two horizontal panes in the same worksheet

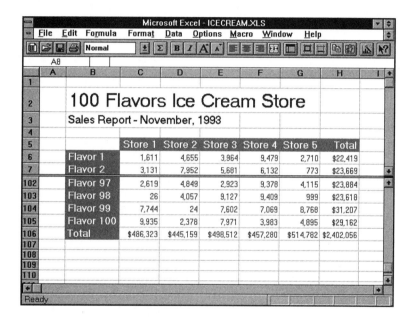

What to do once you've split a worksheet into panes

▼ If cell A1 is the active cell when you choose the Split command, or if the active cell is not in column A and not in row 1 (like if it's in cell E9), Excel will display four panes. To create a two-pane horizontal view, just drag the vertical split bar to the far left side of the worksheet and release it. It will disappear from the worksheet. To create a two-pane vertical view, just drag the horizontal split bar to the top of the worksheet and release it. It will disappear from the worksheet.

continues

▼ Each pane has its own set of scroll bars. You can scroll panes independently to see different parts of the worksheet.

▼ To move back and forth between panes, point and click inside a pane. Or, using the keyboard, press F6 to move the active cell back and forth between panes.

▼ When you create two horizontal panes, the panes scroll together horizontally but not vertically. That's because Excel assumes that you've created two horizontal panes so that you can simultaneously display stuff from the top and bottom of the worksheet.

▼ When you create two vertical panes, the panes scroll together vertically but not horizontally. That's so you can simultaneously see information from the very left and very right sides of a worksheet.

▼ You also can split a window by choosing Split from a worksheet's Control menu. The pointer turns into a four-headed arrow. Position the pointer where you want the split to occur, and click once to split the window into panes.

▼ To remove split panes from a worksheet, open the Window menu and choose the Remove Split command.

Freezing Windows

(Don't put your tongue on 'em)

The Freeze Panes command is extremely effective for fixing titles so that they don't scroll off screen when you scroll through your worksheet

window. For instance, you can freeze the worksheet titles in rows 1 through 5 of the sample worksheet. That way, when you scroll down to see more information, the titles stay in place, but the information below the frozen rows scrolls up toward the top of the worksheet window as usual. This will help you remember what goes in what row as you enter data.

Here's how it works. Position the active cell in column A in the row just below where you want to freeze the worksheet titles. (That's cell A6 in the sample worksheet.) Open the Window menu and choose the Freeze Panes command. Excel splits the window into two panes. The first pane includes rows 1 through 5; the second pane includes everything else in the worksheet.

Now try scrolling through the worksheet. The titles don't move, and the information contained in the worksheet scrolls below row 5.

Rows 1–5 are frozen and will always appear at the top of your worksheet, even if you're in row 99

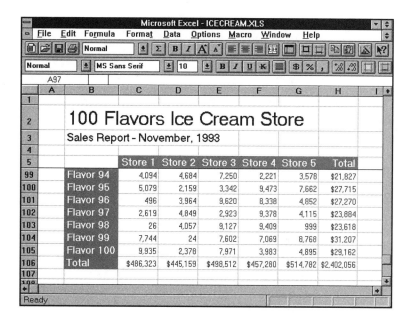

▼ You also can freeze column titles at the left edge of the worksheet. Position the active cell in the first column to the right of where you want to freeze titles in row 1; then choose the Freeze Panes command.

▼ You can freeze column titles and row titles in the same worksheet. It doesn't matter which you create first. Or you can create them at the same time by selecting a cell that's not in column A and not in row 1; then choose the Freeze Panes command.

▼ You can split a worksheet into panes with the Split command and then freeze the top pane, the left pane, or both by choosing the Freeze Panes command.

▼ Unlike the panes created with the Split command, those that Excel creates when you freeze titles do not have their own scroll bars.

▼ To move back into the area that contains the frozen titles, click anywhere in that area or use the arrow keys to move there.

▼ To remove frozen titles from a worksheet, open the Window menu and choose the Unfreeze Panes command.

Who's Zooming Who?

The Window Zoom command. I've never been able to figure out if by selecting this command I'm actually enlarging my worksheet, or simply shrinking myself, my computer, my desk, and everything else in my office. In any case, here are your choices when it comes to shrinking and enlarging your view with the Zoom command.

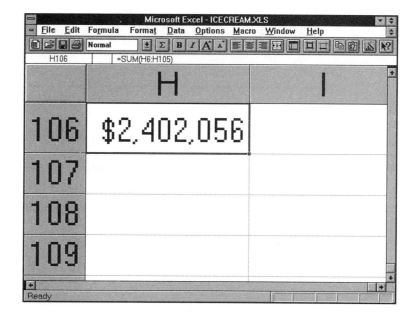

When the boss gripes to you about how small sales have been lately, you can zoom in on the bottom line so that it looks like this

▼ The 200 option doubles the size of your worksheet.

▼ The 100 option displays the normal worksheet size.

▼ The 75 option shows your worksheet at 75% of its normal size. (Of course, this could also mean that you've been enlarged to 125% of your normal size. Do your pants feel tight?)

▼ The 50 option shows your worksheet at 50% of its normal size.

▼ The 25 option shows your worksheet at 25% of its normal size.

▼ The Fit Selection option allows Excel to calculate the optimal zoom factor for a selected worksheet area so that it fits the current window size.

continues

▼ The Custom option lets you make the choice. Type any value from 10 to 400 into the box.

Hiding and Unhiding Windows

Has anyone ever tiptoed up behind you and peered over your shoulder to see what you're doing in Excel? It's almost as if this nosy intruder expects to see your personal statement of net worth or a payroll register listing everyone's salary. Well, it's annoying enough to be tiptoed upon. But when you really *are* working on a personal financial report or the company payroll register, these sneaks can really irritate you. To keep the sneaks from peeking, hide the window.

When you choose the Hide command from the Window menu, Excel immediately removes the active worksheet from your screen. To redisplay the worksheet, open the Window menu and choose Unhide. When the Unhide dialog box appears, click on the name of the worksheet you want to redisplay and click OK. Poof! It's back in an instant. That's pretty much all there is to hiding and unhiding your private worksheets.

"I HATE THIS!"

Hey! Where'd my Window menu disappear to?

When the worksheet you just hid was the only one open in Excel, all the menus except File and Help will disappear from the menu bar. This is normal, so don't panic. Open the File menu and you'll see the Unhide command there. Choose the Unhide command, click on the name of the worksheet in the Unhide dialog box, and click OK to get everything back to normal.

PART III

Formulas for Success

Includes:

CHAPTER 13
Those Fab Functions

IN A NUTSHELL

- ▼ Why you need functions
- ▼ Functions that total a range
- ▼ Functions that can average and count
- ▼ Functions that tell time
- ▼ Functions that make decisions for you
- ▼ Functions that display the N/A message
- ▼ Functions that round off your numbers
- ▼ Functions that make uppercase letters
- ▼ Functions that use a 360-day calendar

CHAPTER 13

In an earlier chapter you figured out how to type basic formulas into a worksheet. These were great for doing things like adding, subtracting, multiplying, and dividing groups of numbers. As your calculation needs get more involved, though, so must your formulas.

The reality of crunching numbers in Excel is that your worksheet is only as smart as you are. You see, when you type a formula correctly, you always get the correct answer. And when you don't, well, you don't. That's the nature of formulas in Excel.

But let's face it, we're not mathematicians. That's why Excel offers a whole slew of built-in formulas, called *functions*. I like to call them the "fabulous functions." And in this chapter we'll take a look at the most fabulous ones around.

TIP

The next chapter covers financial functions—functions that calculate a car loan or home loan payment and other fun things. Don't forget to look at that chapter for other useful functions.

Why Functions?

Functions are invaluable because some worksheet calculations just can't be done easily with those other, basic formulas. Like calculating the sum of the differences of squares of corresponding values in two arrays. (Why would anyone ever want to do that?)

And when it comes to typing them into cells, Excel's functions tend to be more forgiving than the formulas you create on your own. If Excel doesn't recognize the function you're typing into a cell, it'll beep at you. This means, "Nice try, but give it another shot."

Excel catches any typos you make in functions, because each function is designed to do a very specific calculation. When you type a function into a cell, Excel expects to see things in a very specific order—things such as the *arguments*.

BUZZWORDS

ARGUMENT

Arguments are the extra things you type with the function, things that tell Excel which worksheet numbers to crunch.

The basics of entering a function are covered in Chapter 7. Here are the major parts of a function:

▼ The function name is a short, sometimes abbreviated, word that generally describes the function's duty.

▼ The two parentheses are used to separate the function name from the information that you want the function to use in its calculation. You have to type the parentheses.

▼ The arguments—the stuff in parentheses—can be values separated by commas, or cell addresses separated by commas, or a cell range.

SUM Day It'll All Add Up

The SUM function calculates the sum of a group of numbers. It's great to use when you've run out of toes and fingers.

I HATE EXCEL!

The SUM function looks like this:

=SUM(*number1,number2,...*)

Things to remember about using SUM

▼ *number1* and *number2* are the arguments.

▼ You can include up to 30 arguments in a SUM function. That's 30 separate entries separated by commas.

▼ Arguments can be numbers, addresses of individual cells that contain numbers, or cell range addresses that describe where the numbers are.

Examples of SUM

The Function	The Result
=SUM(1,2,3)	**6**
=SUM(C1:C3)	**25**, when C1, C2, and C3 contain 10, 5, and 10
=SUM(C1,D3,F4)	**35**, when C1, D3, and F4 contain 5, 20, and 10

TIP

Don't forget that the AutoSum tool in the toolbar is the quickest way to sum numbers in your worksheets. Just select the range you want to sum, and click on the tool.

Just Your AVERAGE Run-of-the-Mill Function

The AVERAGE function calculates the average of a group of numbers, like the average of six sales figures, the average salary earnings for ten employees, or the average air speed velocity of an African swallow flying into a 30-mph head wind. It's up to you to decide what you want to average.

The AVERAGE function looks like this:

=AVERAGE(*number1,number2,...*)

Examples of AVERAGE

The Function	The Result
=AVERAGE(2,4,6)	4
=AVERAGE(A1:A3)	7, when A1, A2, and A3 contain 10, 4, and 7

Things to remember about using AVERAGE

▼ *number1* and *number2* are the arguments.

▼ You can include up to 30 arguments in an AVERAGE function. That's 30 separate entries separated by commas.

▼ Arguments can be numbers, addresses of individual cells that contain numbers, or cell range addresses that describe where the numbers are.

continues

▼ When figuring out an average, Excel first adds up all the numbers you give to it and then divides that answer by the total number of items you've included in the function.

▼ Excel treats blank cells and zero values differently when it averages numbers. When you include a blank cell as an argument, Excel does not count it as an item when calculating an average. When you include 0—or a cell that contains 0—as an argument, Excel does count it as an item when calculating an average.

Here's an example of using AVERAGE in a worksheet. Notice the different answers Excel comes up with when the cell range contains a blank cell, as opposed to containing the value 0.

Figuring out the average for ranges of numbers in a worksheet

	Microsoft Excel						
File	Edit	Formula	Format	Data	Options	Macro	Window	Help

C16 | =AVERAGE(C6:C14)

BRADY.XLS

	A	B	C	D	E	F	G	H	I
1									
2			The Brady Bunch						
3			Cast Member Favorability Ratings (1 to 10 Scale)						
4									
5			*1973*	*1974*	*1975*	*1976*	*1977*		
6		Mike		2	4	7	5		
7		Carol		0	5	8	5		
8		Greg		0	3	7	10		
9		Marcia	8	0	2	8	10		
10		Jan		2	7	8	4		
11		Peter	8	0	7	9	8		
12		Bobby		0	6	9	7		
13		Cindy		0	9	10	6		
14		Alice	8	2	10	10	6		
15									
16		AVERAGE:	8.0	0.7	5.9	8.4	6.8		
17									
18									

Ready

You Can COUNT on It

The COUNT function counts how many numbers there are in a cell range. This function is helpful for double-checking your work. Suppose that you've just entered today's invoices into a worksheet. You know that there are 282 invoices, but you're not sure whether you actually entered all of them. Use the COUNT function to check it out.

The COUNT function looks like this:

=COUNT(*value1,value2,...*)

Things to remember about using COUNT

▼ *value1* and *value2* are the arguments.

▼ You can include up to 30 arguments in a COUNT function. That's 30 different entries separated by commas.

▼ Arguments can be numbers, addresses of individual cells that contain numbers, or cell range addresses that describe where the numbers are.

▼ If you select a cell range, Excel doesn't count cells that contain text or formula errors.

▼ Excel doesn't count blank cells if they're in a cell range you're using as an argument. (But it does count zeros.)

Here's an example of using COUNT in a worksheet. Notice that Excel ignores the three blank cells and the formula error message when it counts the entries in column C.

Counting the number of entries in a worksheet

	A	B	C	D	E	F	G	H	I	J
1										
2			Invoice Register							
3										
4			#	Date	Acct #	Net	Tax	Gross		
5			234	02/28/93	234	770.06	57.75	827.81		
6				02/28/93	444	942.02	70.65	1012.67		
7			236	02/28/93	212	54.14	4.06	58.2		
8			237	02/28/93	778	886.15	66.46	952.61		
9				02/28/93	566	706.41	52.98	759.39		
10			239	02/28/93	455	10.13	0.76	10.89		
11				02/28/93	534	953.45	71.51	1024.96		
12			#NAME?	02/28/93	99	765.78	57.43	823.21		
13			242	02/28/93	122	158.09	11.86	169.95		
14			243	02/28/93	677	496.89	37.27	534.16		
15										
16		COUNT	6							
17										

C16 =COUNT(C5:C14)

COUNT.XLS — Microsoft Excel

How 'bout a DATE?

Every worksheet wants one; every worksheet needs one. The DATE function is most useful in worksheets that keep track of things by date, but don't necessarily show the parts of the date in a single cell. For instance, an inventory tracking report may show the month, the day, and the year in three different cells. To use the dates in a calculation—say to determine how long an item has been sitting idly in your inventory— you could use the DATE function to join the three.

The DATE function looks like this:

=DATE(*year,month,day*)

Things to remember about using DATE

▼ *year*, *month*, and *day* are the arguments.

▼ The arguments can be numbers or the addresses of individual cells that contain numbers.

▼ Don't use cell ranges as arguments in the DATE function; Excel will display the #VALUE error message in the cell.

Here's an example of using DATE in a worksheet. In this particular version, the function is used to show the expiration date for a perishable inventory item. The expiration date is ten days from the date of purchase.

Keeping track of time with the DATE function

```
┌─────────────────────────────────────────────────────────────┐
│ ─             Microsoft Excel                          ▼ ▲   │
│ File  Edit  Formula  Format  Data  Options  Macro  Window  Help │
│ [icons]  Normal   [Σ B I A A ≡ ≡ ≡ ≡ □ □ □ ▦ ▦ ▧ ▮?]        │
│    H7                 =DATE(F7,D7,E7)+G7                      │
│ ┌──────────────────── DATE.XLS ──────────────────── ▼ ▲ ┐   │
```

	Item #	Description	Month	Day	Year	Max Days On Hand	Toss Out Date
			Date Purchased				
	1	Rose, Samantha	6	3	93	7	06/10
	2	Rose, Sterling	6	3	93	10	06/13
	3	Freesia, Mixed	6	4	93	4	06/08
	4	Alstromeria	6	6	93	5	06/11
	5	Bells of Ireland	6	7	93	5	06/12
	6	Gloriosa Lily	6	9	93	3	06/12
	7	Carnations	6	12	93	12	06/24
	8	Mixed Poms	6	2	93	12	06/14
	9	Mini Carnations	6	1	93	12	06/13
	10	Gyp	6	12	93	14	06/26

Inventory Tracking Report

Ready

The Date and Time Is NOW

The NOW function displays the current date and time in the following format in any worksheet cell: 10/28/93 12:25. This is useful for folks (like me) who have three calendars on their desk, one wrist watch, and two wall clocks, but never seem to remember what time or day it is.

The NOW function looks like this:

    =NOW()

Things to remember about using NOW

▼ This function has no arguments, but you must always include the empty parentheses ( ) after it.

▼ When you forget to place the empty parentheses ( ) after the function, Excel can't recognize the entry and therefore displays the #NAME? error message. Press F2 to edit the entry, type ( ), and press Enter.

▼ The day and time that Excel displays is for the exact moment you typed the NOW function into the cell. To update that entry as time goes on, you must press the F9 function key to recalculate your worksheet.

▼ The date and time that Excel displays comes from your computer's internal clock. Be sure that your computer's clock is correctly set when using the NOW function in your worksheets.

▼ Use the NOW function in formulas to figure out things like how many days have gone by between now and when you last paid a vendor, or between now and when a client purchased something from you.

Collect $200 Only IF You Pass Go

The IF function is one of the most useful Excel functions. It lets you ask questions about things and then take different courses of action, depending on the answer you get. The power of the IF function is extended when you combine it with other functions, like the SUM function.

The IF function looks like this:

=IF(*logical_test***,***value_if_true***,***value_if_false***)**

Things to remember about using IF

▼ *logical_test*, *value_if_true*, and *value_if_false* are the arguments.

▼ The *logical_test* argument is a value or a question that has a true or false answer. For instance, if you want to ask the question, "Is the value in cell C5 greater than or equal to 450?" you would type **C5>=450** for this argument. Or you can ask the question, "Is 500 equal to the value in cell B9?" by typing **500=B9** as the argument. The questions you ask in the IF function can include any of the following *comparison operators*:

This operator	*Means…*
=	Equal to
>	Greater than
<	Less than
>=	Greater than or equal to
<=	Less than or equal to
<>	Not equal to

continues

Things to remember about using IF, continued

▼ The *value_if_true* argument tells Excel what to do if the answer to the question is TRUE.

▼ The *value_if_false* argument tells Excel what to do if the answer to the question is FALSE.

▼ The "what to do" aspect to using the IF function means many things. To tell Excel to calculate a formula and display the result, type the formula as you normally would. To display a few descriptive words in a cell, type the text within quotation marks.

In the following sample worksheet, notice the IF function in cell D3. The function looks at the number in B3. If it is equal to 100, Excel displays `Perfect Score` (the *value_if_true* argument). If B3 doesn't equal 100, Excel displays `Good Try` (the *value_if_false* argument).

Use the IF function to ask questions and then give direct answers about information in your worksheets

	Microsoft Excel	
File **Edit** **Formula** **Format** **Data** **Options** **Macro** **Window** **Help**		

		Normal	Σ B I A' A'

D3	=IF(B3=100,"Perfect Score","Good Try")

	IF.XLS							
	A	B	C	D	E	F	G	H
1								
2								
3		98		Good Try				
4		100		Perfect Score				
5								
6								

Sorry, I'm NA Quite Ready

Use the NA function to display `#N/A` in any cell (that is, any cell used in a formula) that doesn't currently contain information, but soon will. This message means "no value available." Any formulas that reference

this function will display #NA! rather than a zero. This would alert your worksheet readers that the information is a coming attraction.

The NA function looks like this:

=NA()

Things to remember about using NA

▼ This function has no arguments, but you must always include the () after it.

▼ When you forget to place the () after the function, Excel can't recognize the entry and therefore displays the #NAME? error message. Press F2 to edit the entry, type (), and press Enter.

▼ You can type **#N/A** directly into a cell. Excel treats this entry exactly as if you had typed in the NA function.

Let's Just ROUND It Off a Bit

The ROUND function gets rid of all those unsightly numbers to the right of a decimal place. In some worksheet reports, it's just not politically correct to show decimal-place values; for instance, imagine how a Fortune 500 sales figure like $283,451,229.02 would look in an annual report. Not kosher.

With the ROUND function, you can round a number to a certain amount of digits. Rounded numbers do not change in their cells; the original numbers are still used in all the calculations. Only what's displayed on your screen changes.

The ROUND function looks like this:

=ROUND(*number,num_digits*)

Things to remember about using ROUND

▼ *number* and *num_digits* are the arguments.

▼ The *number* argument is the number you want to round.

▼ Arguments can be numbers or the addresses of individual cells that contain numbers.

▼ The *num_digits* argument is the number of digits to round by. If this value is greater than 0, Excel rounds to that many digits to the right of the decimal point. If this value is equal to 0, Excel rounds to the nearest integer. If this value is less than 0, Excel rounds to that many digits to the left of the decimal point.

Examples of ROUND

The Function	The Result
=ROUND(567.891,2)	567.89
=ROUND(567.891,0)	568
=ROUND(A1,A2)	570, when cell A1 contains the number 567.891 and cell A2 contains the number −1

UPPER-Case Appeal

The UPPER function converts text characters to all uppercase characters. At first glance, you might look at a feature like this and say to yourself, "Oh, come on! Why not just retype it?" Good point. But when your boss asks you to change a 27-word report title, the UPPER function's appeal will suddenly dawn on you.

The UPPER function looks like this:

=UPPER(*text*)

Things to remember about using UPPER

▼ *text* is the only argument.

▼ The argument can be text, enclosed in quotation marks, that you type as part of the function, or it can be the address of an individual cell that contains text.

Examples of UPPER

The Function	The Result
=UPPER("stuff")	STUFF
=UPPER(C5)	STUFF, when cell C5 contains the word *stuff*

TIP

Once you've converted text with UPPER, you may want to get rid of the function itself, leaving the appropriately cased text behind. Here's how. Select the cell that contains the UPPER function. Click on the Copy tool in the toolbar. Now open the Edit menu and choose the Paste Special command. In the Paste Special dialog box, click on the Values button and then click OK. Once Excel returns you to the worksheet (the marquee should still be showing around the cell), press Enter. Excel converts the UPPER function into its displayed value (even though the "value" really is text).

I'm How Many DAYS Late on That Payment?

Bankers, financiers, and accountants often use a 360-day calendar. Where did those extra 5 days disappear to? The fact is, this calendar was invented because no one likes dividing by 365 or having to remember the leap years. This shorter calendar assumes that there are 30 days per month and 12 months per year, for a total of 360 days per year.

Excel uses a 365-day calendar whenever you perform calculations on dates in a worksheet. When your business reports and accounting system are based on a 360-day calendar, you can use the DAYS360 function to determine the "actual" number of days between two points in time.

The DAYS360 function looks like this:

DAYS360(*start_date,end_date*)

Things to remember about using DAYS360

▼ *start_date* and *end_date* are the two arguments.

▼ The arguments can be date numbers or the addresses of individual cells that contain date numbers.

▼ You also can type the arguments as dates surrounded by quotation marks, as in **"12/09/93"** and **"5/01/95"**. But when you use DAYS360 this way, don't use cell addresses to refer to the cells that contain the arguments; type the text, surrounded by quotation marks, directly into the cell with DAYS360. If you use cell ranges as arguments, Excel will display the #VALUE error message in the cell.

▼ You can enter a formula as an argument. For instance, if you type **5** as the start date and **7+8** as the end date, Excel treats the end date as 15 and displays the answer 10.

▼ When *start_date* is after *end_date*, the DAYS360 function gives you a negative answer.

▼ The DAYS360 function is particularly useful for computing the number of days late a customer's payment is. Many businesses use "aging" reports to organize late payment information according to the number of days late: 0 to 30 days late, 31 to 60 days late, and 61 to 90 days late.

I HATE EXCEL!

Examples of DAYS360	
The Function	**The Result**
DAYS360(C1,D1)	**31**, when cell C1 contains the date 09/23/93 and cell D1 contains the date 10/24/93
DAYS360(C1,D1)	**360**, when cell C1 contains the date 09/23/93 and cell D1 contains the date 09/23/94

TIP

If you're worried about the negative impact on your finances of using a 360-day calendar, you needn't worry too much. Unless you're computing the interest that's due you on a $5,000,000 loan you gave to a friend, the difference between computing with a 365-day and a 360-day calendar is negligible.

CHAPTER 14

Functions You'll Profit From

IN A NUTSHELL

▼ "If I borrow x amount of money at x interest rate for x number of years, what will my monthly payments be?"

▼ "If I can afford to pay x amount of money each month at x interest rate for x number of years, how much can I borrow?"

▼ "If I owe x amount of money at x interest rate, how many payments of x amount do I have to make?"

▼ "How much interest did I pay on that loan?"

▼ "If I save x amount of money at x interest rate, how much money will I have in x years?"

▼ "If I want to have x amount of money in x years, how much do I have to save each month at x interest rate?"

CHAPTER 14

In the last chapter we came to grips with the fact that we aren't mathematicians, which is exactly why those fabulous functions are so handy. In this chapter we make another startling revelation: we're not stockbrokers either.

Even so, with a little background material and your fine typing skills, you can learn how to produce some useful information about your finances by using Excel's financial functions. You can get answers to questions like these: "How long should I invest this money to end up with a billion dollars?" and "What's the total interest paid on my yacht loan last year?" and "How can I buy real estate with no money down?"

CAUTION

Your worksheet is only as smart as you are. Typing the right numbers into your financial functions can mean the difference between making money and losing it—in your worksheet, anyway. (Here comes the disclaimer.) That's the nature of investing. Just be sure that you understand the information that the financial functions give you, always triple-check your numbers, and don't ever bet your life savings on a sure thing. Finally, never forget the first rule of investing: you can always bury the cash in your backyard.

If you can't remember how to enter a function, turn to Chapter 7 for a quick review.

Why Financial Functions Are Special

There are three important rules to understand about financial functions before you use them in your own worksheets. Here they are, spelled out for you in plain, non-technical English sentences.

▼ Don't mix year units with month units with day units. For example, to figure out the monthly payment on a mortgage, be sure to type the *monthly* interest rate and the total *months* for the loan.

▼ Any money amount that goes out of your pocket must be typed as a negative number. That includes things like deposits you make in a bank, payments you make on a loan, and checks you write to buy stocks and bonds. Money that comes back into your pocket (that's the best kind) are positive numbers.

▼ Any argument that I call "optional" is just that, optional. You don't have to enter a value for the function to return a correct answer. So don't make up numbers just for the heck of it.

Financial Arguments

Excel's financial functions use pretty much the same arguments. This makes it easy to work with them. You don't have to learn a whole new set of arguments for each one. Here's the hit list:

▼ *fv* is the future value of the investment. When somebody offers to pay you an amount of money ten years from now if you invest today, that future amount is the investment's future value.

▼ *nper* is the total number of payment periods. A 30-year home mortgage, for instance, has 30 annual payments and 360 monthly payments. (Don't get this one confused with *per*.)

continues

▼ *per* is a number that corresponds to a particular payment period. For instance, to get principal and interest information for the fifth year in a 10-year loan, you would use the number 5 for this argument. (Don't get this one confused with *nper*.)

▼ *pmt* is the payment you make each period. This amount typically includes principal and interest, but does not include fees like documentation charges or taxes. When you're the one who's making the payments, use a negative number to show that the money is going out of your pocket. When someone else is making the payments to you, use a positive number to show that the money is flowing into your pocket.

▼ *pv* is the value of an investment at this very moment. When someone asks you to deposit a lump sum of money into a bank today, that sum would be considered the present value of the investment.

▼ *rate* is the interest rate earned or paid per period. When you enter the rate, you have to match the rate term to the number of payments in the period. Usually you do this by dividing the rate by the payment term. For example, for an annual interest rate of 12% and 12 monthly payments, you'd enter **.12/12**. That's the same as a monthly interest rate of 1%.

▼ *type* is an optional argument that describes when payments are made. Use the number 1 for payments you make at the beginning of the period, or the number 0 for payments you make at the end of the period. If your payments are due at some other interval, omit this argument. Excel will assume that it's an end-of-period payment.

I HATE EXCEL!

▼ *guess* is an optional argument. It's your best guess of the per-period interest rate. I know, it sounds funny that you should guess about anything that has to do with money. Don't worry. Excel simply uses the guess to make a calculation go more quickly. It has to do with the way some financial calculations work. In any case, the value you type will in no way impair the function's accuracy.

▼ If you want to skip an optional argument that's in the middle of the argument list, you must enter the comma to let Excel know that you're skipping it.

TIP

Here's an easy way to let Excel type your function arguments for you. For any function, type everything up to and including the first (left) parenthesis into the formula bar. Then press Ctrl+A. Excel automatically types the necessary argument descriptions for you into the formula bar. The first of these always is highlighted. Now edit each description, replacing the text with the number needed to complete the function. When you're finished doing this, type the ending parenthesis and press Enter to display the answer in your worksheet.

How Much Is That Loan Payment?

The PMT function is most commonly used to figure out what your payment will be on a loan. For instance, you can use this function for home or car loans.

The PMT function looks like this:

=PMT(*rate,nper,pv,fv,type*)

Things to remember about using PMT

▼ *rate*, *nper*, and *pv* are the required arguments.

▼ *fv* and *type* are optional arguments. If you leave out *fv*, Excel assumes a value of 0. If you leave out *type*, Excel assumes that you're making end-of-period payments.

▼ Arguments can be numbers or the addresses of individual cells that contain numbers.

Suppose that you want to purchase your dream house with a mortgage amount of $250,000 and a flat-rate mortgage of 30 years at 10%. Here's the formula:

=PMT(.1/12,30*12,250000)

Because you are making monthly payments, you have to convert the interest rate and term to months. The monthly interest rate, for example, is equal to .1/12. The actual number of payments you'll make is 360 (12 payments for 30 years). The result is $-2,193.93.

TIP

The best way to work with the function is to type the variables (the stuff that can change) into cells and then use cell references in the function. That way you can change the interest rate or the amount of the loan and see the effect on the payment. Here's an example:

TIP

Cell	Enter	What it means
A1	.1	rate
B1	30	nper (term)
C1	250,000	pv (amount of loan)
D1	=PMT(A1/12,B1*12,C1)	function

TIP

Another way to figure loan payments is to ask yourself, "If I can afford car payments of $300 a month at .9% interest for 4 years, how much can I afford to borrow?" The next section helps you with this one.

A different twist on this function is to figure out how much money you need to save to reach a certain amount. For instance, suppose that you want to save $12,000 in 8 years at an interest rate of 6% annually. How much should you save a month? Use a different set of arguments, like this:

=PMT(.06/12,12*8,,12000)

The extra comma between the *pv* and *type* arguments tells Excel that there's no entry for the *fv* argument. Without this extra comma, Excel would not be able to return the correct answer of $-97.90. (A negative number indicates that the money comes out of your pocket, remember?)

How Much Money Can I Borrow?

Another way to figure a loan payment is to start with the amount of money you can afford to spend each month and then work backward to the amount you can afford to borrow. To do this, use the PV function.

Here's what the PV function looks like:

=PV(*rate,nper,pmt,fv,type*)

Things to remember about using PV

▼ *rate*, *nper*, and *pmt* are the required arguments.

▼ *fv* and *type* are optional arguments. If you leave out *fv*, Excel assumes a value of 0. If you leave out *type*, Excel assumes that you're making end-of-period payments.

▼ Arguments can be numbers or the addresses of individual cells that contain numbers.

Suppose that you can afford car payments of $300 a month, and the current annual interest rate is 9%. You want a 4-year loan. Use this function:

=PV(.09/12,4*12,-300)

The answer is $12,055.43.

If you want to enter the rate, term, and payments in cells, you might have something like this:

Cell	Enter	What it means
A1	.09	*rate*
B1	4	*nper* (term)
C1	-300	*pmt* (payment)
D1	=PV(A1/12,B1*12,C1)	function

EXPERTS ONLY

Read this if you have money to invest

If you are big on investments, use the PV function in a different way to figure out the present value of an investment. This function can evaluate the worth of an investment in terms of today's dollars. If the investment payoff is worth more than $0 in terms of today's dollars, then the investment is worth it. However, if the worth of the investment today is less than $0, it's a money loser. You're better off investing in something else.

Suppose that you're looking into purchasing a life insurance policy that offers an investment feature. You can buy the policy today for $25,000. The policy earns an annual interest rate of 8% and returns to you a $250 monthly payment for the next 15 years. Is this a good investment?

The function you'd type into the worksheet looks like this:

=PV(.08/12,15*12,250)

EXPERTS ONLY

The answer you get is $26,160.15. This means that the value in terms of today's dollars of receiving $250 per month for 15 years is $26,160.15. Since you can buy that "worth" today for only $25,000, it's a good deal.

How Many Payments Do I Have To Make?

The NPER function tells you how many payments you have to make on a given loan. Here's what the NPER function looks like:

=NPER(*rate,pmt,pv,fv,type*)

Things to remember about using NPER

▼ *rate*, *pmt*, and *pv* are the required arguments.

▼ *fv* and *type* are optional arguments. If you leave out *fv*, Excel assumes a value of 0. If you leave out *type*, Excel assumes that you're making end-of-period payments.

▼ Arguments can be numbers or the addresses of individual cells that contain numbers.

Suppose that you're considering borrowing some money to buy a car. A friend has offered to loan you $15,000 at an annual interest rate of 15%. (What a pal, huh?) The friend wants you to make monthly payments of $557.51. How long will it take you to pay off the loan?

The function you'd type into the worksheet looks like this:

=NPER(.15/12,-557.51,15000)

It would take you exactly 33 months to pay off the loan.

What's the Interest Rate I Need?

The RATE function calculates the periodic interest rate for a loan or investment. Here's what the RATE function looks like:

=RATE(*nper,pmt,pv,fv,type,guess*)

Things to remember about using RATE

▼ *nper*, *pmt*, and *pv* are the required arguments.

▼ *fv*, *type*, and *guess* are optional arguments. If you leave out *fv*, Excel assumes a value of 0. If you leave out *type*, Excel assumes that you're making end-of-period payments.

▼ Arguments can be numbers or the addresses of individual cells that contain numbers.

Let's fantasize that your local yacht dealer offers you a 5-year, $40,000 loan with monthly payments of $899. You go across town to the competition to price-shop, but you forget to bring the other quote along. You can't remember what interest rate you were quoted on the other loan. (Loan people are great at giving you the monthly amount, but they sometimes don't tell you the interest rate, unless you ask. This function

will come in handy in these cases, too.) The second dealer will give you the same $40,000 loan at an annual interest rate of 13%. Which loan is better?

The function you'd type into the worksheet to find out the first dealer's interest rate looks like this:

=RATE(5*12,–899,40000)

The answer you get is 1.04%. This is the *monthly* interest rate because the period is monthly. You must multiply this by 12 to get the annual rate of 12.45%.

Here's What I'm Really Interested In

The IPMT function tells you how much interest you paid during a single period of a loan. At tax time, for instance, your accountant will ask you how much interest you paid on your mortgage during the previous year. This function will tell you:

=IPMT(*rate,per,nper,pv,fv,type*)

Things to remember about using IPMT

▼ *rate*, *per*, *nper*, and *pv* are the required arguments.

▼ *fv* and *type* are optional arguments. If you leave out *fv*, Excel assumes a value of 0. If you leave out *type*, Excel assumes that you're making end-of-period payments.

▼ Arguments can be numbers or the addresses of individual cells that contain numbers.

Here's an example of how to use IPMT. Suppose that you need to determine how much interest you paid during the third year of a 5-year loan. The loan is structured so that you make one loan payment per year, at the beginning of the year. The annual interest rate for this $100,000 loan is 12%. What's the interest amount you paid for year number three?

The function you'd type into the worksheet looks like this:

=IPMT(.12,3,5,100000,,1)

The extra comma between the *pv* and *type* arguments tells Excel that there's no entry for the *fv* argument. Without this extra comma, Excel would not be able to return the correct answer of $-7,138.84 (the negative sign means that the money's going out of your pocket).

Now imagine that you'd like to figure out the interest you paid during the last month of a $50,000 5-year loan. For this loan, you make 12 end-of-month payments each year. The annual interest rate is 10%. The function you'd type into the worksheet looks like this:

=IPMT(.10/12,60,5*12,50000)

The *per* argument value comes from the fact that the number of the last month in a 5-year loan would be 60 (5*12). The correct answer is $-8.78.

Here's the Principal Thing I'm Interested In

The PPMT function tells you how much principal you paid during a single period of a loan. This is a handy figure to know should you ever want to pay off a loan early. Just figure out how much you've paid on the principal. Then subtract that amount from the original loan, and that's

what's still due on the loan. (Be sure to check with your loan shark about pre-payment penalties on the loan. You might decide to keep both the loan and your fingers for a while longer.)

Here's the function:

$$=PPMT(rate,per,nper,pv,fv,type)$$

Things to remember about using PPMT

▼ *rate*, *per*, *nper*, and *pv* are the required arguments.

▼ *fv* and *type* are optional arguments. If you leave out *fv*, Excel assumes a value of 0. If you leave out *type*, Excel assumes that you're making end-of-period payments.

▼ Arguments can be numbers or the addresses of individual cells that contain numbers.

TIP

You can also use the IPMT function, discussed a couple of pages ago. The IPMT and PPMT functions use the same arguments. When you're evaluating the same period (that means the per argument must be the same for both), you place these two functions side-by-side in a worksheet. One will show the interest paid for that period; the other shows the paid principal. Now add them together and you get the total loan payment for that period.

Here's an example of how to use PPMT. Suppose that you need to determine how much principal you paid during the third year of a 5-year loan.

The loan is structured so that you make one loan payment per year, at the beginning of the year. The annual interest rate for this $100,000 loan is 12%. What's the principal amount you paid for year number three?

The function you'd type into the worksheet looks like this:

=PPMT(.12,3,5,100000,,1)

The extra comma between the *pv* and *type* arguments tells Excel that there's no entry for the *fv* argument. Without this extra comma, Excel would not be able to return the correct answer of $17,629.89.

Now add this value to the one you got from the IPMT example presented earlier in this chapter:

Principal	-17,629.89
Interest	-7,138.84
Total loan payment, yr. 3	$-24,768.73

EXPERTS ONLY

Creating a loan payment schedule with IPMT and PPMT

With home mortgages and other amortized loans, the amount of the loan payment each period is the same. That means your payment amount in year 1 is exactly the same as in year 2, year 3, and so on. But lenders love to get their money as soon as possible. That's why when they chop up the earlier loan payments into principal and interest, the interest portion is always much higher than the principal portion. The IPMT and PPMT functions show exactly how things are chopped up for any period during the life of the loan. You therefore can create a table of amounts that shows how principal and interest are distributed over the life of the loan. (Take a look at the sample worksheet on the next page.)

Creating a loan
amortization
schedule for your
mortgage

```
┌─────────────────────────────────────────────────────────────┐
│ □                    Microsoft Excel                   ▼ ▲  │
│ File  Edit  Formula  Format  Data  Options  Macro  Window  Help │
│ [▣][🗁][🖫][🖨] Normal    [↕][Σ][B][I][A][A'] [▤][▤][▤][▤] [□][□][□][📋][📊][📈][▨][▶?] │
│        D8          │ =IPMT(C3,C8,C4,-C2,,1)                   │
│ ┌──────────────────── AMORTIZE.XLS ──────────────── ▼ ▲ │  │
│ │   A    B       C       D        E        F       G  │▲  │
│ │ 1                                                   │   │
│ │ 2  Loan Amount $100,000                             │   │
│ │ 3  Interest Rate  12.00%                            │   │
│ │ 4  # of Years      5                                │   │
│ │ 5                                                   │   │
│ │ 6                                                   │   │
│ │ 7            Yr.   Interest  Principal  Balance     │   │
│ │ 8             1      $0.00  $24,768.73  $75,231     │   │
│ │ 9             2   $9,027.75 $15,740.97  $59,490     │   │
│ │ 10            3   $7,138.84 $17,629.89  $41,860     │   │
│ │ 11            4   $5,023.25 $19,745.48  $22,115     │   │
│ │ 12            5   $2,653.79 $22,114.93      $0      │   │
│ │ 13                                                  │   │
│ │ 14                                                  │   │
│ │ 15                                                 ▼│   │
│ │ ◄│                                              │► │   │
│ Ready                                                       │
└─────────────────────────────────────────────────────────────┘
```

What'll It Be Worth Tomorrow?

The FV function tells you what an investment will be worth some day in the future. This is the type of investment where you make equal monthly deposits into an account for a fixed period of time. The FV function looks like this:

=FV(*rate,nper,pmt,pv,type*)

Things to remember about using FV

▼ *rate*, *nper*, and *pmt* are the required arguments.

▼ *pv* and *type* are optional arguments. If you leave out *pv*, Excel assumes a value of 0. If you leave out *type*, Excel assumes that you're making end-of-period payments.

I HATE EXCEL!

▼ Arguments can be numbers or the addresses of individual cells that contain numbers.

Here's an example of how to use FV. Suppose that you're saving for your child's college education. He is expected to start college (hopefully) in 8 years. You can afford to take $100 out of your paycheck each month and deposit it into a savings account. The account pays 6% interest annually. What's the amount in the account at the end of 8 years?

The function you'd type into the worksheet looks like this:

=FV(.06/12,8*12,-100)

Because you are making monthly payments into the account, you'll have to convert some units to months. The monthly interest rate, for example, is equal to .06/12. The actual number of deposits you'll make into this bank account over 8 years is equal to 96 (8*12).

At the end of 8 years, the account will be worth $12,282.85. (You might have to send Junior to a state school.) But suppose that the savings account already contains $5,000 when you start making the monthly deposits. What will it be worth in 8 years? Here's how the function should look:

=FV(.06/12,8*12,-100,-5000)

The answer you get is $20,353.57. That extra $5,000 in the account at the beginning sure makes a big difference!

TIP

If you want to tinker with the figures (the interest rate, the payments, and so on), enter the arguments into cells and then use cell references in the formula. For instance, you can enter the following:

Cell	Enter	What it means
A1	.06	rate
B1	8	nper (term)
C1	-100	pmt (payment)
D1	=FV(A1/12,B1*12,C1)	function

Then you can change the values in A1, B1, and C1 to see how the changes affect the formula's results in D1.

Will I Really Make Any Money?

The NPV tells you what the net present value is for an investment. Net present value is a tool you can use to evaluate the worth of an investment in terms of today's dollars. Here's the rationale. If the investment payoff is worth more than $0 in terms of today's dollars, then the investment's worth it. However, if the worth of the investment today is less than $0, it's a money loser. You're better off investing in something else.

Here's what the NPV function looks like:

$$=NPV(rate, value1, value2...)$$

▼ *rate* and *value1* are the required arguments.

▼ The *value1* argument generally is a cell range that contains the series of cash flows (the money you pay out and the money you get back over the life of the investment).

▼ *value2* is the optional argument. It is used as payment and income, like *value1*.

▼ The NPV calculation is for future cash flows. If your first cash flow occurs at the beginning of the first period, the first value must be added to the NPV result, not included in the values argument.

▼ Arguments can be numbers or the addresses of individual cells that contain numbers. The *value1* argument usually is a cell range address.

The easiest way to get a feel for the NPV function is to look at a worksheet that lays out three investment scenarios. In this example, the competing rate of interest on the projects is 13%. But as you can see, the flow of money back to you differs greatly from project to project.

I HATE EXCEL!

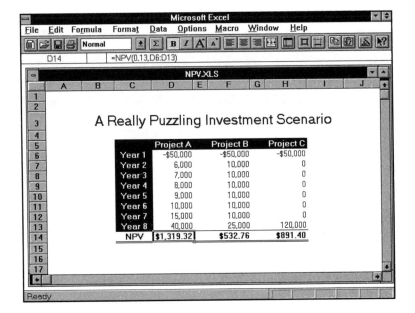

Evaluating the
worth of three
different invest-
ments by com-
paring their net
present values

Microsoft Excel

File　Edit　Formula　Format　Data　Options　Macro　Window　Help

Normal

D14　　=NPV(0.13,D6:D13)

NPV.XLS

A Really Puzzling Investment Scenario

	Project A	Project B	Project C
Year 1	-$50,000	-$50,000	-$50,000
Year 2	6,000	10,000	0
Year 3	7,000	10,000	0
Year 4	8,000	10,000	0
Year 5	9,000	10,000	0
Year 6	10,000	10,000	0
Year 7	15,000	10,000	0
Year 8	40,000	25,000	120,000
NPV	$1,319.32	$532.76	$891.40

Ready

The final decision is made by choosing the project that has the greatest net present value. That's the one (in terms of today's dollars) that'll put more money in your pocket over the long haul. Looks like Project A is the winner.

218

PART IV

Graphs and Databases

Includes:

CHAPTER 15

You Say Chart, I Say Graph

IN A NUTSHELL

▼ Creating a chart with the ChartWizard tool

▼ Editing a chart

▼ Saving a chart

▼ Formatting a chart

▼ Printing a chart

E very time you open a newspaper or flip through a magazine, you see all sorts of graphic images. These images are trying to tell you something. They're trying to "inform" you visually without forcing you to read tables full of words and numbers.

Excel charts present your worksheet numbers graphically. Charts usually make numbers easier to understand. Sometimes they even uncover trends and patterns that aren't obvious by looking at the numbers themselves. Bottom line, given the choice between viewing a chart or reading a text report, people will take charts every time.

This chapter shows you the quickest way to turn any group of worksheet numbers into an appealing and informative chart.

All You Really Need To Know about Charts

There are several different ways to create charts in Excel, and each one gets you to the same end result. Of all the methods, only one has enough appeal that you'll use it over and over again: the ChartWizard tool. It's the next-to-last button at the right end of your toolbar, just left of the Help tool. (The ChartWizard tool is the one with the magic wand waving over the bar chart. I know, it's looks like a bunch of smokestacks.)

Creating charts with ChartWizard is painless and effortless because you don't have to memorize lots of confusing steps. ChartWizard takes you by the hand and leads you step-by-step through the chart-creating jungle (lions, and tigers, and bears, oh my).

BUZZWORDS

CHART VS. GRAPH

Most people don't know the difference between a chart and a graph. I'm one of them. Every software program I've ever worked with uses the term "graph" to describe any colorful picture that's based on numbers. But for some strange reason, Excel uses the term "chart" to describe what we call a graph.

Chart Magic with the ChartWizard

You can't use the ChartWizard tool unless you have a mouse. If you have a mouse but are reluctant to use it, now's the time to get over your bashfulness.

Here's how to create a chart by using the ChartWizard tool:

1. Highlight the cell range in your worksheet that contains the numbers you want to include in your chart. Be sure to include the column headings and row headings if you want to show them as well.

I HATE EXCEL!

```
┌─────────────────────────────────────────────────────────────┐
│ ─                        Microsoft Excel                 ▼ ▲ │
├─────────────────────────────────────────────────────────────┤
│ File  Edit  Formula  Format  Data  Options  Macro  Window  Help │
├─────────────────────────────────────────────────────────────┤
│ [▣][☞][▨][⬛] Normal    [▼][Σ][B][I][A̅][A̲][▤][▥][▦][▧][▨]... │
├─────────────────────────────────────────────────────────────┤
│        B5                                                     │
├─────────────────────────────────────────────────────────────┤
│ ─                          INVEST.XLS                    ▼ ▲ │
│     A      B        C       D       E       F      G      H    I │
│  1                                                            │
│  2        Invest In Your Future                              │
│  3        Portfolio Breakdown                               │
│  4                                                           │
│  5                     Jan     Feb     Mar     Apr    May    Jun │
│  6        Stocks      6,026   2,714   2,681   5,032  4,209  6,856 │
│  7        Bonds         164   1,411   8,673   9,137  4,872  5,007 │
│  8        Money Market  446   9,229   5,283   6,802  9,663  5,065 │
│  9        Commodities 2,169   1,705   8,095     622  3,972  7,610 │
│ 10        Market Value: $8,805 $15,059 $24,732 $21,593 $22,716 $24,538 │
│ 11                                                           │
│ 12                                                           │
│ 13                                                           │
│ 14                                                           │
│ 15                                                           │
│ 16                                                           │
│ 17                                                           │
├─────────────────────────────────────────────────────────────┤
│ Ready                                                         │
└─────────────────────────────────────────────────────────────┘
```

The highlighted cell range in this worksheet is the one that's going to be charted

2. Click on the ChartWizard tool in the toolbar.

The familiar marquee appears around the worksheet range you selected.

3. Drag your mouse to select the worksheet area where you want Excel to put the chart. The size of the area you drag through determines how big the chart will be. Don't worry, Excel won't overwrite any cell information with the chart. Excel stacks the chart on top of your worksheet. You can easily move the chart aside (perhaps to reveal data underneath it) by dragging it aside.

Excel displays a dialog box called "ChartWizard Step 1 of 5" and shows the address of the cell range you selected in step 1.

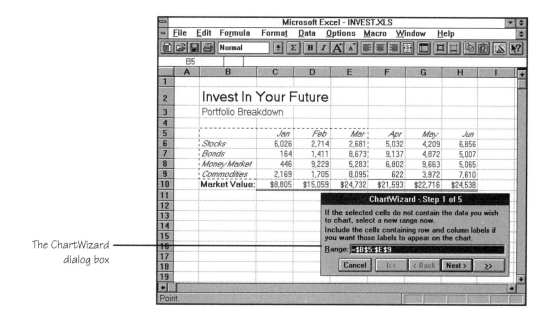

The ChartWizard dialog box

4. If the range is OK, click on the Next button. If you need to, change the cell range you selected (maybe you forgot to include a row or column of numbers in step 1) by typing the new cell range address into the Range box. To be sure that you're typing in the correct cell range, you might have to drag the ChartWizard dialog box out of the way. When you're finished, click on the Next button to continue.

A dialog box with Excel's fourteen chart categories appears. This is ChartWizard Step 2 of 5.

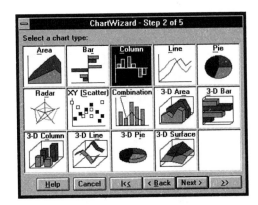

Excel offers fourteen different categories of charts, from pie to column to 3-D

5. Click on the chart category that looks closest to the one you want to create. Don't worry if it's not exactly what you're looking for. You can customize it or even change your mind and pick a new category later. If you're not sure, don't pick anything. Keep the chart that Excel has picked for you. When you're finished, click on the Next button.

A dialog box appears with the various formats for the chart category you selected. This is ChartWizard Step 3 of 5.

6. Click on the chart format that looks closest to what you want to create. If you're not sure, don't pick any of them. Excel picks one for you. When you're done, click on the Next button.

The next dialog box displays a sample of your chart. This is ChartWizard Step 4 of 5. For the most part, everything you do in this dialog box can stay as is. Excel is pretty good at choosing the right settings for you.

7. At this point, you might decide to use a different chart format or chart category. To do so, click on the Back button until you get back to the correct dialog box (you're looking for ChartWizard Step 2 of 5 or Step 3 of 5). Make the change; then click on the Next button until you're back in ChartWizard Step 4 of 5.

When you're happy with how your chart looks, click on the Next button to continue. The next dialog box, ChartWizard Step 5 of 5, displays the same sample of your chart and gives you a chance to add a title.

8. To add a title to your chart, click inside the Chart Title box and type the title you want to show at the top of your chart. When you're happy with how your chart looks, click OK.

At this point, Excel sends you back to your worksheet. The chart you created now appears as an embedded object. It's size should match up exactly to the size of the cell range you selected in step 3. Notice the small boxes that appear all around the perimeter of the chart object; these are *handles*. Whenever the handles appear, it means that the object has been selected and that Excel is ready for you to do something to it.

Excel sticks the chart in your worksheet

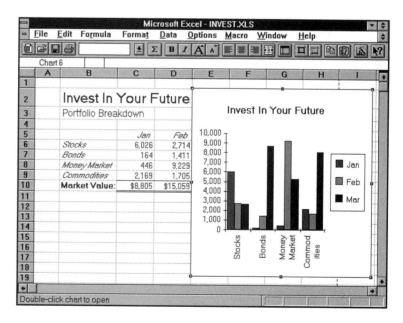

I HATE EXCEL!

OBJECT

Excel allows you to create and then insert objects into a worksheet. These objects range from simple geometric shapes to fully detailed charts. (You just learned how to create and insert a chart, which is an object.) When you insert an object into a worksheet, you're "embedding" that object, also called an "embedded object."

"I HATE THIS!"

My chart is all smunched! What gives?

If your chart is all squished up, don't worry. You didn't select a large enough area for your chart. You'll find out how to fix it in the next section, "Tinkering with the Chart."

CAUTION

You can quickly delete an embedded chart from any work-sheet by clicking on the chart once and then pressing the Del key. But be careful. When you delete a chart this way, you can get it back if you choose the Edit Undo command before doing anything else. When that doesn't work, you must re-create the chart with the ChartWizard to display it again.

As you begin looking at your own worksheets to figure out what data you want to chart, keep the following range-selecting tips in mind:

Checklist

▼ When highlighting the worksheet range you want to chart, always include the row and/or column containing the words that describe your data. When you do this, Excel creates a legend box for your chart and adds text descriptions to the chart's horizontal axis.

▼ If rows and columns contain SUM functions or any other formulas or functions that calculate totals-type data, leave them out of your cell range selection. Excel charts are designed to help a viewer get a visual feel for the totals represented in your numbers. You don't need to chart your totals data to do that.

Here are some navigational techniques you can use while you work in the ChartWizard:

Checklist

▼ The Next button advances you to the next step in the process. Once you make a selection inside a dialog box, click on this button to continue the process.

▼ The Back button backs up a single step in the process. This is useful for returning to a previous step so that you can review a selection you made there.

▼ The >> button immediately creates a chart using whatever options you've selected up to that point in time. (This button is for impatient chart-makers.)

▼ The << button takes you all the way back to when you opened the ChartWizard dialog box. Whenever a chart you've created is too bizarre-looking for words, you might want to use this button to start the process over again.

▼ The Cancel button stops the current ChartWizard sequence and sends you back to your worksheet. This is useful if you suddenly realize that you're working in the wrong worksheet. Cancel the process, open the other worksheet, and start over again.

EXPERTS ONLY

Read this if you wanna know what goes where, and why

After you play around a bit, you'll notice that Excel will chart some cell ranges differently than others. Sometimes Excel deals with your worksheet range in terms of rows of data, so that each row of numbers appears as one data grouping in the chart. Other times, Excel uses columns of data as individual groupings. In both cases, it's easiest to think of these data groupings as "data series." That's the term Excel likes to use.

The choice that Excel makes about how to create the data series from your worksheet range determines what goes where on your chart. In the sample chart, for instance, there are three different data series. The data series names appear in the legend box and are color-coded to help you see which bars in each investment grouping belong to the Jan data series, the Feb data series, and the Mar data series.

The easiest way to identify the data series in an Excel chart is to look at the names in the legend box. For a ChartWizard chart that doesn't have a legend, just look under the Data Series In heading in the ChartWizard Step 4 of 5 dialog box. Whichever button is pressed shows you how Excel created the data series for your chart.

Tinkering with the Chart

ChartWizard inserts its chart into your worksheet. Now that it's embedded, what do you do with it?

Checklist

▼ To select a chart object so that handles (those teensy boxes) appear around its perimeter, click once anywhere inside the chart.

▼ Click anywhere outside a selected object to "deselect" it. The handles will disappear.

▼ To move the chart, select it and then drag it with your mouse. Click and hold anywhere inside the chart object; then drag the mouse in the direction you want to move the chart. When you're there, release the mouse to reposition the object.

▼ To resize the chart, drag any of its handles in the direction you want to resize.

▼ To change the data used in the chart, just edit the worksheet. When you change the worksheet numbers in an embedded chart, Excel quickly redraws the chart to show the new numbers. This means that you can actually watch Excel update the embedded chart the second after you change a number in the worksheet.

Changing the Chart

Unless your last name is da Vinci, rarely will your charts start out looking like the Mona Lisa. That means you'll want to make changes to it. Perhaps you want to delete numbers from the chart. Or maybe you'd like to use a more descriptive title.

To edit a chart, click on it once to select it. Then click on the ChartWizard tool. Excel displays the familiar ChartWizard dialog box and offers you the opportunity to edit your chart in two easy steps.

"I HATE THIS!"

I thought there were five steps in ChartWizard!

Just when you figured out how to do the ChartWizard 5-Step, you edit an embedded chart and discover the ChartWizard 2-Step. It's not as complicated as it first seems. Just remember that whenever you're editing an embedded chart this way, Excel shows only two of the five dialog boxes you see when you're creating a chart by using the ChartWizard.

Editing a chart with ChartWizard

▼ In ChartWizard Step 1 of 2, you can chart a different set of data: either type a new cell range in the Range box or use your mouse to select the new range in the worksheet (the cell range address automatically appears in the Range box). When you're finished, click on the Next button.

▼ In ChartWizard Step 2 of 2, you can change how your chart numbers are organized. For example, click on the Rows button under "Data Series in" so that each row of worksheet numbers gets grouped together in a series; or click on the Columns button so that each column of numbers gets grouped together in a series. Feel free to experiment on your own graphs by clicking on these two buttons.

▼ When you're finished editing the chart, click OK to return to the worksheet. Your changes will be reflected in the embedded chart.

Saving Your Chart

Once you've created a chart, or shortly after you've made a few changes, you'll want to make a permanent copy of it.

Saving and opening charts

▼ When you save a worksheet that contains an embedded chart, Excel saves both the worksheet data and the chart data in a worksheet file.

▼ When you use the Open command from the File menu to open a worksheet that contains an embedded chart, both the worksheet and the embedded chart appear together.

▼ When you choose Save from the File menu while a chart is occupying its own window, Excel creates a "chart file." A chart file is separate and different from a worksheet file. When you create a chart file, Excel adds .XLC to the end of the chart name. A chart that's in its own window can also be embedded in a worksheet, but it's not required. (Double-click on a chart to put it in its own window.)

▼ To display a chart you saved in a chart file, first use File Open to open the worksheet that contains the numbers used in the chart. Then use File Open to open the chart.

EXPERTS ONLY

Sneaking a chart open

You're allowed to open a chart into Excel without opening the worksheet that contains its data. When you do, Excel will show a message asking whether you want to "Update references to unopened document?" (Translation: Do you want to

EXPERTS ONLY

show the chart even though the worksheet that has the chart's numbers isn't open?) If you click on Yes, Excel looks into the worksheet on-disk and gathers up the most recent numbers; then it shows the numbers in your chart. (If the worksheet has been deleted, Excel displays the File Not Found dialog box.) If you click on No, Excel doesn't check unopened documents for changes in data and gives you the chart as it was when you last saved it.

Formatting a Chart

Formatting a chart is similar to formatting a worksheet. You can make a chart look glamorous, or you can keep it simple. The two most common formatting activities are changing the chart type and customizing the look of your chart. You also can add a legend and title to your chart, if the ChartWizard didn't add them already. The title(s) and legend help orient a reader to the information in your chart.

Things to keep in mind when formatting a chart

▼ To start, double-click on the chart object embedded in your worksheet. This puts the chart in its own window.

▼ Whenever a chart is displayed in its own window, the menus change. The Format menu contains commands that work specifically with charts.

▼ The commands you use to add objects to your charts (stuff like legends, titles, and arrows) are located on the Chart menu.

▼ Whenever you make a mistake or change your mind about a feature you just added to a chart, use the Edit Undo command to undo it, or press Ctrl+Z.

Changing the Chart Type

What if you want to change your chart's type, such as changing a column chart to a 3-D bar chart? You can. Open the Gallery menu, which displays the name of all the chart categories available to you. Click on the name of the chart you want to use. Excel displays the Chart Gallery dialog box, which shows all the types of charts available for the category you selected. When you find the one you want to use, click on it and then click OK.

TIP

Another way to change the chart type is to click on the type you want in the Chart toolbar displayed at the bottom of the screen. This toolbar automatically appears whenever you embed a chart object in your worksheet. The first 17 tools on this toolbar correspond to the different types of Excel charts.

Bestowing Titles (And other meaningful text)

A chart title is just like a worksheet report title. You show it at the top of your chart. People who read the chart can get a good idea about its contents simply by scanning your title. When you're not sure that one

title is enough to get the point across, add another one. In Excel, the first title is known as the chart title. The second title is just called text. (Hey, some titles are official-sounding, others aren't.)

If you didn't add a chart title when you created the chart, you can add one now. Open the Chart menu and choose the Attach Text command. When Excel displays the Attach Text dialog box, click on the Chart Title button (it may already be selected) and then click OK. Excel displays a title marker (with the word "Title" in it) at the top of the chart. At this point you can begin typing the title. When you're finished, press Enter and Excel will enter the title into the chart. Press Esc to remove the marker from around the title text.

Now suppose that you want to add a second title to the chart. This time you won't choose a command from a menu. Instead, just start typing the text. When you're finished, press Enter. Excel shows the text you typed inside a marker in the center of the chart. But that's probably not the greatest place to show the title, so move it just below the chart title by dragging it there with your mouse. When you're finished, press Esc to remove the marker from around the text.

A Legend in Its Own Mind

A legend is a color-coded (or pattern-coded) visual object that's designed to help a reader understand the information in your chart. If the worksheet cell range you charted contains row headings and columns, Excel automatically shows a legend at the right side of a chart. But if you didn't include headings in the selected range, you might want to add a legend later.

To add a legend to the chart, open the Chart menu and choose the Add Legend command. Excel creates a legend—complete with dummy descriptions, like Series1 and Series2, or "guesses"—and inserts it into your chart. To make the dummy series names into more descriptive legend text, you have to follow a second set of steps.

Open the Chart menu and choose the Edit Series command. The Edit Series dialog box appears. You'll see Excel's guesses or the same dummy names listed in the Series box. Click on the first dummy name, click inside the Name box, type a real name, and then click on the Define button. Click on the second dummy name, click inside the Name box, type a real name, and then click on Define. Continue this process until all the legend names have been added. When you're finished, click OK to return to the chart window. Press Esc to remove the marker from around the newly edited legend.

Now, to reposition the legend in the chart, select the legend by clicking on it. Open the Format menu and choose the Legend command. Click the button next to the position you want to use. Excel offers five choices: Bottom, Corner, Top, Right, and Left. Normally Excel places the legend on the right side of the chart. When you've selected a position button, click OK to move the legend.

TIP

An easier way to reposition the legend is simply to drag it to the exact spot in the chart where you want it to appear.

Objects of Desire (Making chart objects pretty)

Anything you can do to text in a worksheet can be done to text in a chart. Need to make the font bigger? Simple enough. Want to choose a new typeface? No problem. You'd love to align stuff differently? Go right ahead.

The great part about formatting in a chart window is that you can change the appearance of just about anything. This includes stuff like bar colors, pie slice patterns, legend boxes, and much more. Just remember, always start by selecting the object you want to format. When the handles appear around the object, you can do one of the following two things.

Checklist

▼ Open the Format menu. Any command you can use for formatting that object is black; those that don't apply are dimmed (gray). While inside a formatting dialog box, choose your options; then click OK to apply your selections to the chart.

▼ Right-click on the object with your mouse. This displays the shortcut menu. Only the commands you can use to format that particular object are on this menu. While inside a formatting dialog box, choose your options; then click OK to apply your selections to the chart.

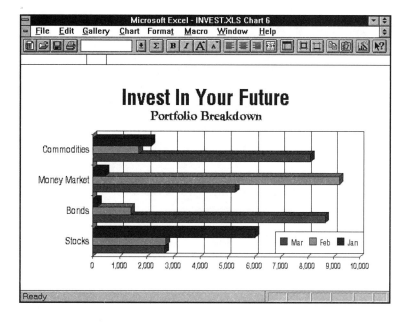

The final, format-
ted version of
the chart

TIP

Double-clicking on most objects inside the chart window
displays the Patterns dialog box for that object. In addition
to containing the formatting options you'd expect to see,
these dialog boxes sometimes contain other buttons. The
other buttons are named things like Font and Legend. By
clicking on these buttons, you can quickly move from one
formatting dialog box to another. This "backdoor" eliminates
the need to exit one dialog box and then select another
formatting command to get to another dialog box.

Printing a Chart

Printing a chart is just as easy as printing a worksheet. In fact, you use the same command: File Print. What actually appears on the printout, however, will depend on where in Excel you are when you choose the File Print command.

To print only the chart, move the chart into its own window. If it's currently displayed as an embedded object, double-click on it. Now open the File menu and choose the Print command. Click OK to print the chart.

To print the chart and the worksheet in which it's embedded, make sure that the worksheet is in the active window. Click on the worksheet to make it active. Now open the File menu and choose the Print command. Click OK to print the worksheet and the chart.

TIP

To exert a bit more control over the printing process, you can play around with the dialog box options in the Print dialog box. You also can change the page layout for your chart by using the settings in the Page Setup dialog box. For more information about both of these dialog boxes, go back and read Chapters 6 and 11.

CHAPTER 16
Dynamic Databases

IN A NUTSHELL

- ▼ Creating a database
- ▼ Editing a database
- ▼ Sorting information
- ▼ Managing a database with the Data Form
- ▼ Searching for specific types of information

Excel has an alter ego. You're already familiar with the Excel that lets you analyze facts and figures in a worksheet—the one that makes it easy to spiff up a worksheet, save it, and then print it out. All really cool, useful features.

The "other" Excel lets you organize data like a database program. What if you want to create a list of business contacts? Or perhaps you want to organize your daily invoices. Maybe you'd like to create a mailing list for your company's telemarketing division. You don't have to spend gobs of money on complex database programs like dBASE or Paradox. You can gather, store, and reorganize monster-sized collections of information in an Excel worksheet.

BUZZWORDS

DATABASE PROGRAM

A database program is a program designed to work with related sets of data. Using the database program, you can enter, sort, find, and list data in many different ways.

This chapter exposes Excel's alter ego. You'll discover that working with a database is just like working with a worksheet. (Hey, they're the same thing!)

A Few Terms To Gnaw On

Terminology, buzzwords, and ominous acronyms. I hate them, and maybe you do, too. But before we begin data-ing our bases, let's go over a few of the important terms. As you read each one, keep one eye glued to the sample database shown in the following figure. Things will make a lot more sense to you while you read.

	A	B	C	D	E	F	G

Candy Bar Database

Field names →

NAME	COST	CALORIES	EATEN
Butterfinger	$0.50	750	45
Milky Way	$0.75	655	23
Snickers	$0.75	712	76
Kit Kat	$0.45	439	50
Mars	$0.50	475	12
Reese's	$0.65	500	135

Field →

Record →

Stuffy-sounding terms

▼ A *database* is an electronic file. You can type information into it, shuffle the information around, and then pull things back out in lots of different ways.

▼ In a worksheet, a *database range* is the cell range where you actually keep your information.

▼ A *record* is everything that's on one row in a database. A record contains one set of information about a person, place, or event. For instance, a record in an address database might list a person's first and last name, address, city, state, ZIP code, and phone number.

continues

▼ A *field* is one little chunk of information in a record. Each chunk, such as a last name, an address, or an invoice number, sits in its own cell.

▼ A *field name* is the name that sits atop each column in your database. It describes the chunks of data in that column. A column that contains first names, for example, might use the word FIRST for its field name.

Creating a Database

What kind of facts and figures do you want to collect in your database? How do you want to be able to get that information back out? These are the two most meaningful questions to ponder as you sit down to create your first database.

In terms of what information your database will contain, ask yourself some questions: "Do I want to store the names and addresses of my business contacts?" "Do I need to keep track of how many different brands of candy bars I eat each week?" Whatever your ideas, you might want to sketch them out on a piece of paper. (Believe me, it'll help to preserve your sanity later on.) You don't have to write down all the individual entries for your database. Just jot down some words that you think would work well as field names.

As for what you want to get back, be sure that each piece of information you want to manipulate is in its own field. For instance, if you want to be able to sort by state, be sure to enter the state as a separate field (in its own cell), rather than use one field for both city and state.

Typing into a Database

Type your field names into the worksheet. Do so in an order that makes sense to you. In a candy bar database, for instance, the first field name might be NAME, the second COST, the third CALORIES, and the fourth EATEN. You're simply typing words into a worksheet, so feel free to use anything you've remembered from earlier chapters to edit or change your entries. Continue doing this until you've entered all your field names.

Then move one row down and start typing the bits and pieces of data that belong to the first record. Move down another row to type in the second record, another row for the third record, and so on. Typing records into a database is exactly the same as typing words and numbers into a worksheet. Use the same common sense you normally follow for entering text, numbers, dates, and times.

Good things to remember when you're building a database

▼ The first row in a database always contains the field names.

▼ When you type a field name into the worksheet, be sure that Excel recognizes it as text (as opposed to a number, a formula, or a pterodactyl). The entries NAME, PHONE#, and TOTAL1 are good examples of words that meet this requirement. The entries 500, 01/25/93, and 8:00 are examples of the kinds of entries to avoid. Also, avoid using formulas or function names for your field names.

▼ Keep your field names short and sweet. Shorter field names are easier to work with and easier to remember.

▼ The number of field names at the top of the database should always match the number of individual chunks of info in a record. Four field names, four chunks per record. Thirty field names, thirty chunks.

continues

CHAPTER 16

Good things to remember when you're building a database, continued

▼ It's okay to enter incomplete records into a database. Just leave the cell blank where that missing chunk of info belongs.

▼ Don't enter records that have more chunks of information than there are field names. Either reduce the number of chunks for that record, or add new field names for the extra chunks.

▼ Excel's not particular about how you capitalize words in your records or in the field names at the top of the database. As far as Excel's concerned, the entry **SMITH** and **smith** are the exact same thing.

Putting on the Database Hat

Typing records is the most time-consuming aspect to working with a database. But once it's full of useful information, you're ready to go. The next thing to do is tell Excel that it's a database. (This is where you unleash Excel's alter ego.)

Here's all you need to do to tell an Excel worksheet that it's now a database:

1. Using your mouse, select all the cells in the database range. Be sure to include the row that contains the field names, too.

2. Open the Data menu and choose the Set Database command.

As soon as you do this, Excel takes off its worksheet hat and puts on its database hat. (It's one of those Jekyll and Hyde things.) Now look in the Reference area at the left end of the formula bar. You should see the word *Database* there. Excel names the cell range you selected; that way, Excel always knows where your database begins and ends in the worksheet.

246

TIP

Include a blank row at the bottom of the database range. This makes it easier (as you'll soon see) to add more information to the database later.

Changing Your Database

Your databases will need to change. You can count on that because information changes. People relocate to new addresses, business contacts get promoted, new candy bars hit the market, and so on. Once you create a database and enter records, be prepared to make a few changes sometime in the future. The most typical kind of change becomes necessary when you want to add a new record or change a chunk of information in an existing record. Another kind of change becomes necessary when you want to add more chunks of information to what's already available in the database. Both are easy enough to do.

Changing a database is exactly like changing a worksheet. There aren't any special tricks to learn.

Checklist

▼ To add new records to your database, just type them, starting in the first blank row at the bottom of the database. Then use the Set Database command (Data menu) to tell Excel where the new database range is located.

▼ When you need to squeeze a new record in between two other records, use the Edit Insert command.

continues

I HATE EXCEL!

Checklist, continued

▼ Want to delete a record that's no longer needed? Use the Edit Delete command to delete the row.

▼ You can use any of the formatting commands to format a database so that it looks more presentable when you include it in a report.

TIP

If you keep a blank row at the bottom of your database, entering new records is even easier. Start by using the Edit Insert command to insert blank rows between the row that contains the last record and the blank one you keep at the bottom of the database. This allows Excel to automatically expand the cell range you've defined as the database range. After you type in the new records, you're done! There's no need to use the Set Database command again, because you inserted the new records inside the newly expanded database range.

CAUTION

Anytime you add new information that falls outside of the original area you defined as the database, be sure to use the Set Database command to let Excel know about it. This is really important when it comes time to locate records in your worksheet. For example, suppose that you enter a new record in row 50. But the last time you told Excel about your database, the database range only went up to row 49. Until you use the Set Database command again, Excel will never be able to find the information in row 50.

The A to Z's of Arranging Records

The one thing you can do in a database that just can't be done easily in other programs is quickly rearrange things lots of different ways. When you rearrange records in a database, you are "sorting" information. You might want to list your address database in alphabetical order. Or, if you are doing a mailing, you might want to sort the database by ZIP code. There are lots of ways to sort your data with Excel.

The Key to the Sort

To sort a database, you need to choose a *sort key*. You can select any cell in the column you want to use for the sort key. In your database, for example, column B might contain the last name, column C the address, column D the ZIP code, and so on. To sort by last name first, you'd choose column B as your sort key.

BUZZWORDS

SORT KEY

A sort key identifies the column that contains the information you want to sort.

Excel lets you pick as many as three sort keys at a time. This is really helpful when the first field you are sorting contains the same entry. For instance, you might know a lot of Smiths. Let's imagine that the address database contains 200 records, and you want a list of all the Smiths that live in Utah. If you sort just by last name, there might be quite a few records for Smith. Even when they're all sorted together in a group of rows, it'd take quite a long time to locate the information you want.

So what you do is choose a second sort key—the column that contains the state. Then you tell Excel to sort first by last name, second by state.

Sorting

Here's how to sort an Excel database:

select total field to be sorted

1. Select the range of cells that contains the records you want to sort. Be sure to *exclude* the row that contains the field names.

It's really important to exclude the field names row from your selection. When you include it, Excel thinks it's a record. You don't want to sort this row into your database, as if it were just another record.

2. Open the Data menu and choose the Sort command.

Row or col only that you wish to sort by.

Excel displays the Sort dialog box. Notice that a marquee appears around the first cell in the first row of the range you selected. This cell's address also appears in the 1st Key box. Excel starts by assuming that you want to use the first column as your sort key.

3. Choose the column you want to use as the first sort key. To do this, click on any cell in that column. (If you can't see your database, drag the dialog box out of the way.) The selected cell's address will pop into the 1st Key box. You also can type the cell address inside the 1st Key box.

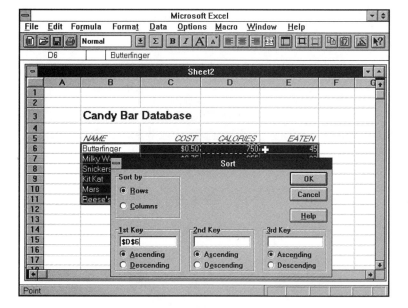

Clicking on cell D6 identifies column D as the first sort key, as shown in the 1st Key box in the Sort dialog box

4. If necessary, choose the second sort key. Click once inside the 2nd Key box; then click on the cell in the column you want to use as the second sort key. Excel pops that cell's address into the 2nd Key box. If you don't want a second sort key, skip ahead to step 6.

5. If you want, choose the third sort key. Click once inside the 3rd Key box; then click on the cell in the column you want to use as the third sort key. Excel pops that cell's address into the 3rd Key box. If you don't want a third sort key, skip to the next step.

6. Click on the Ascending button below any sort key box to sort stuff in a top-to-bottom fashion. This sorts letters in an A-B-C order and sorts numbers in a 1-2-3 order.

Or click on the Descending button below any sort key box to sort stuff in a bottom-to-top fashion. This sorts letters in a C-B-A order and sorts numbers in a 3-2-1 order.

7. Click OK to sort the database.

Excel sorts the database according to the sort keys you chose in the Sort dialog box.

"I HATE THIS!"

I added new records, and now everything is all out of sorts again!

If you add records after you have sorted your database, you have to re-sort it to get the new records in the right places. Sorry.

Undoing a Sort Operation

When you don't like what you see after Excel sorts your database, you can undo the sort operation. Just open the Edit menu and choose the Undo command. Keyboard nuts can press Ctrl+Z. Remember, you have to do this immediately after you sort the database, or you won't be able to return it to its original order.

As a final option, use the File Close command to close the worksheet (but DON'T save your changes); then use File Open to reopen it. This last-ditch, drastic measure will bring back the database in the same order it was in the last time you saved it by using the File Save command.

EXPERTS ONLY

Order in the database! Order in the database!

If you need to keep track of the order in which you entered records into the database, you should insert a column to add a field for record numbers. In this field, enter 1 for the first record, 2 for the second record, and so on. Then, if you sort a

EXPERTS ONLY

database lots of different ways and want to get back the original entry order for the records, you can just use the record number column as the first sort key.

Cruising Your Database with Data Form

Excel lets you use something called the "Data Form" to view your database. The Data Form makes it a breeze to work with any database, simplifying its uses in ways that you will truly appreciate. The Data Form makes it a breeze to work with any database. When you display the Data Form for a database, you can view one record at a time, edit a bunch of records, and add or delete records. You also can tell Excel to show only the records that have similar characteristics.

To use the Data Form, you first must be sure to tell Excel where your database range is located. Use the Set Database command to do this. Now open the Data menu and choose the Form command. Excel displays the Data Form for your database. You'll recognize the information that Excel shows in the Data Form, because it comes right from your database.

Here's the Data Form for the candy bar database

▼ The Data Form shows one record at a time and each field within that record. In the upper right corner of the Data Form, Excel displays the current record number and the total number of records in the database. This is called the "record number indicator."

▼ The Data Form can work with any size database you create in a worksheet. When your database range contains 5 fields, for instance, the Data Form is fairly small on your screen. When your database range has 15 fields, Excel stretches the size of the Data Form to show as many of the fields as possible.

▼ Click on the scroll bars to move from record to record in your database.

▼ Click on the Find Prev or Find Next button to show the previous or next record, respectively, in the database.

▼ To edit the contents of any record, display it as the current record in Data Form. You can press the Tab key to move from field to field in a record. Each time you move to a new field, Excel highlights the information in that field. You can either type over the existing entry or edit it. When you're finished editing in a field, press Enter to store the new information in that field.

▼ Click on the Restore button to cancel any changes you've made to the current record. Excel goes back out into your database and retrieves the original information. Once you've pressed Enter to make a change in a field, you can't use Restore to get the original field entry back. Sorry.

▼ Click on the New button to add a new record to the database. Type in each entry, and press Tab to move from field to field. When you're finished creating the new record, Excel adds it to your database.

▼ Click on the Delete button to delete the current record. Excel will display this message: `Displayed record will be deleted permanently.` Click OK to delete the record, or Cancel to keep it.

▼ Click on the Close button to close the current Data Form and return to the worksheet.

CAUTION

Be extremely careful when you use the Delete button. Once you delete a record from your database, it can't be restored. Not even with the Edit Undo command.

Finding Records

You can be really picky about which records are shown in a Data Form. This makes it easier to work with large databases. You won't have to scroll through thousands of records to find information in just a few. Just tell Excel the rules, or "criteria," and Excel will do the matching.

BUZZWORDS

CRITERIA

Criteria are the scientifically formal (or formally scientific) descriptions for what the rest of us call "rules." These rules tell Excel how to find stuff in a database. You could concoct a rule that says, "Find every record in the database that has the word 'Elvis' in the NAME field." Excel would immediately look inside your database and locate every occurrence of Elvis.

Match-Maker, Match-Maker, Make Me a Match

First, open the Data menu and choose the Form command to display the Data Form for your database. To create your rules, click on the Criteria button. Excel displays what looks like a blank record. But look closely. Notice that the word *Criteria* appears where you usually see the record number indicator. At this point you can begin typing your rules into the boxes. For instance, if you want to search for a particular name in your database, just type that name into the NAME field. Or, if you want to search for a particular age, type that number into the AGE field.

When you're finished typing your criteria, click on the Find Next button to locate the first record that meets your conditions. Click on the Find Next and Find Prev buttons to go back and forth between records that meet the criteria. When you're finished looking through the database, click on the Form button to return to the Data Form.

Close Enough

You also can find matches that fall within a certain range or category. For example, let's say that you want to find all records with a sale price less than $50. In the PRICE field, type **<50** and then click on the Find Next button. You also can use comparison criteria with dates and times.

Comparison symbols you can use to search through a database

▼ Use **>** to search for numbers that are greater than some number.

▼ Use **<** to search for numbers that are less than some number.

▼ Use **>=** to search for numbers that are greater than or equal to some number.

▼ Use **<=** to search for numbers that are less than or equal to some number.

▼ Use **<>** to search for numbers that are not equal to some number.

PART V

That's the Way
I Like It
(Customizing Excel)

Includes:

CHAPTER 17

The Miracle of Macros

IN A NUTSHELL

- ▼ Demystifying macros
- ▼ Recording a macro
- ▼ Playing back a macro
- ▼ Changing a macro
- ▼ Saving a macro
- ▼ Thinking about some macro ideas

Macro. This seemingly innocuous word is the most menacing of all computer terms. The second that someone suggests that you use a macro or (gasp!) create one, dark clouds begin to form overhead and lightning bolts fall from the sky. By the time the smoke clears away from the top of your computer, you feel like you just survived a week full of Friday the 13th's.

Look, it's really not that dramatic. Maybe you haven't heard, but a macro is supposed to make using Excel easier—not harder. A macro is a tool you use to automate your favorite worksheet activities; it's not the ultimate computer jinx. So if creating and using a macro even remotely resembled black magic, I'd be the first one to warn you. Heck, I'd be the first one out the door.

This chapter shows you how easy it is to create and use macros. If you've ever used a tape recorder before, you already understand about 50% of what Excel macros are all about.

Demystifying Macros

The mysterious macro. What exactly does it do? What does one look like? Do you need an IQ over 200 to create one or to use one? The fact of the matter is that a macro is just a list of instructions. You give the instructions to Excel, and Excel follows them. In most cases, the instructions are no more complicated than those you'd give to a buddy who's driving across town to visit you. Go to the first light and turn left; it's the third house on the right side of the street. Starting from cell A1 go three rows down and four columns to the right; then draw an outline border.

BUZZWORDS

> **MACRO**
>
> The word "macro" has been around for about 35 years now. This term actually is an abbreviation of "macroinstruction," which refers to a single computer instruction that stands for a sequence of operations. In Excel, this sequence of operations can mean a whole set of formatting steps, printing steps, or even database sorting steps. You get to decide which worksheet operations are included in your macros.

Let's take a look at some of the most often-asked questions about macros. After reading these, you'll be ready to make a little magic of your own.

What's So Special about a Macro?

A macro's instructions guide Excel to perform many of the same worksheet tasks that you'd normally do by hand—stuff like typing data into a cell, moving around the worksheet, changing fonts, drawing lines, and so on. It's like having a maid around to take care of your worksheets for you.

The real benefit to using a macro is that it saves you time. Let's face it, most of the stuff you do in Excel takes more than a step or two to do. Every time you want to format something, you have to go through the same old rigmarole of opening the Format menu, choosing a command, clicking option buttons, and typing in text boxes. All this before you even get to click OK to actually accomplish something. A macro can do all that stuff for you.

Where Do Macros Live?

Macros live in one of two places. First, you can keep a macro on a *macro sheet*. A macro sheet is a special Excel document that looks exactly like a worksheet, except that the cells contain *macro functions* that tell Excel what to do. Instead of using the three-letter extension XLS at the end of its file name, macro sheets use the letters XLM. (Yup, the M stands for *macro*.) To run a macro that's on a macro sheet, that macro sheet has to be open. You take care of opening and saving the macro sheets you need.

BUZZWORDS

MACRO FUNCTION

Each instruction in a macro is called a "macro function." That's because they look a lot like the functions you use to calculate numbers in your worksheet. A macro function starts with an equal sign, followed by a descriptive name, and then a set of arguments that tell the function exactly what to do. Here's the macro function that applies the Currency format to a cell, with no decimal places:

=FORMAT.NUMBER("$#,##0;-$#,##0")

But don't worry. You don't have to type all that garble. Excel does it for you.

The other place that a macro can live is in the *global macro sheet*. This sheet is just like a regular macro sheet, except that the macros you store on the global macro sheet are available in all worksheets. Excel takes care of opening and saving this worksheet. Normally this worksheet is hidden.

What Can My Macros Do?

Normally, you wouldn't create a macro to perform an activity that's already easy to do, such as adding bold or italic style to text. You can use the toolbar tools to do this type of thing. But suppose that you have a particular color shading pattern that you use in many of your worksheets. Every time you want to use this pattern in a worksheet, you have to perform the same seven steps:

1. Select the cells to be formatted.

2. Open the Format menu.

3. Choose the Patterns command.

4. Select the pattern style from the Pattern list.

5. Select the first color from the Foreground list.

6. Select the second color from the Background list.

7. Click OK to add the pattern to the selected cells.

Wouldn't you like to be able to highlight a range of cells and press only two keys to accomplish the same thing? In this case, a macro lets you do in two steps what normally would take seven steps to do!

Macros are ideal for storing instructions for your favorite Excel activities. These are the ones that you find yourself using over and over again. You can create macros that help you move around and edit your worksheets, format data, print a cell range, sort a database, and more.

I HATE EXCEL!

Your First Recording Session

(Jamming with Fleetwood Macros)

There are two ways to create a macro. Assuming that you speak Excel's macro language fluently, you can create a macro by typing the instructions into a macro sheet. But that's not likely.

By far the easiest way to create a macro is to record it. And no, you don't have to speak macro-ese to do it. Excel has a recording feature that, when turned on, keeps a record of every keyboard tap and mouse click you make. You can store this recording on a macro sheet and then play it back.

TIP

If you're not certain about which choices you might make, hold a dress rehearsal. Open a new, blank worksheet and perform the exact steps that you want to automate. As you go through this dry run, write down the menu and command names.

Starting the Recorder (Lights, Camera...)

To record a macro, start by opening a new, blank worksheet into Excel. Now open the Macro menu and choose the Record command. As soon as you do, Excel displays the Record Macro dialog box. To personalize your macro, you can change the settings in the Record Macro dialog box: you can type a new macro name, and you can create a shortcut key that will start the macro.

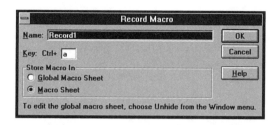

The Record
Macro dialog box

First, type the name of your macro into the Name box. Excel starts by suggesting the name *Record1* here, but you can use any name you want. Be inventive and descriptive. Come up with a name that's sure to always remind you of what the macro's designed to do. For example, use the name *Pattern* for a macro that uses the Patterns command to shade your worksheet cells.

Second, inside the Key box, type the letter you want to use as the shortcut key. Excel starts by displaying the letter *a* here, but you can use any letter you want. Capitalization matters! For example, Ctrl+P and Ctrl+p are two different shortcut keys. The letter *p* would make sense for the pattern macro.

Third, click on the Global Macro Sheet button in the Store Macro In block.

EXPERTS ONLY

Global vs. regular ol' macro sheet

The global macro sheet is a hidden macro sheet that opens every time you start Excel on your computer. Its name is GLOBAL.XLM. The advantage to storing macros in the global macro sheet is that they're always available to you—regardless of the worksheet that's open in Excel. Some macros are ideal for the global macro sheet, such as the ones you think you'll use on any worksheet. The most common kinds are editing and formatting macros. A database sorting macro may not be a great candidate for the global macro sheet,

EXPERTS ONLY

simply because not every worksheet you create has a data-base that needs to be sorted. You might want to store this type of macro in a regular macro sheet.

If you store a macro in a regular macro sheet, you have to be sure to save and name the macro sheet. When you want to use or edit the macro sheet, you have to open it first.

Finally, click OK to turn on the recorder. Excel returns you to the worksheet, ready for you to begin opening the menus and choosing the commands you want to record in the macro. The word *Recording* appears in the status bar at the bottom of your screen until you turn off the recorder, which you learn next.

Recording Your Actions (Action!)

Next, you complete the steps you want in your macro. Just choose the menu commands and options as you normally would. Excel records each choice you make. Don't worry if you make mistakes while you're recording, you can always go back later and edit the macro.

Using the Pattern macro as an example, let's say that you want to add a colored pattern to the active cell in your worksheet. Open the Format menu and choose the Patterns command. Then click on the down arrow next to the Pattern list box to open it. Click on a pattern in this list, such as the sixth style. Next click on the down arrow next to the Foreground list box to open it. Click on the color you want, perhaps red. Then click on the down arrow next to the Background list box to open it. Click on another color, such as yellow. Finally, click OK to return to your worksheet and apply the colored pattern.

When you are finished recording your selections, open the Macro menu and choose the Stop Recorder command. Excel turns off the macro recorder and removes the *Recording* message from the status bar.

This sample recording session shows you how to record a macro that adds a colored pattern to any group of worksheet cells, but you literally can record anything you want. Instead of cell shading, how about the steps for changing a font typeface and point size? Or the steps for drawing a double-line under a cell? Or the steps that do all three of these things at once? It's completely up to you, and that's the beauty of the miraculous macro.

Playing Back the Macro

Now you're ready to test out the macro you just recorded. Just move to a different cell in your worksheet and press Ctrl+p. Excel immediately adds the same pattern to that cell. You can continue moving to other cells in the same worksheet and pressing Ctrl+p to add the pattern there. Now try selecting a range of cells and pressing Ctrl+p. The shading appears in every cell in that range.

TIP

If you can't remember your macro's shortcut key, you can choose the macro name from a list. Open the Macro menu and choose the Run command. In the Run Macro dialog box, click on the name of the macro you want to run. The name is listed in the Run box. Then click OK to run the macro.

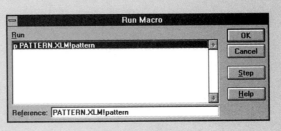

Changing Instructions in a Macro

You'll occasionally press the wrong keyboard key or mis-click your mouse while you're recording a macro. It happens to all of us at one time or another. When you record things in a macro that really don't belong there, you can simply rerecord the macro.

Follow the same steps you did when you began creating the macro. Be sure to type the same name in the Record Macro dialog box. When you click OK, Excel will warn you that a macro with that name already exists and will ask whether you want to overwrite the macro. Click Yes and then rerecord the steps. Go slow this time and get it right!

Creating Additional Macros

(More fun!)

To record another macro, just follow the same steps you did to create the first one. Excel will add the macro to the global macro sheet.

CAUTION

Although Excel is pretty good with macro names, it's not too good with shortcut keys. Suppose that you record another macro and give it the same shortcut key you gave the other one. Guess what happens? Excel goes along happily as if nothing's wrong.

When more than one macro uses the same shortcut key, the macro whose name appears first alphabetically will run when you press that shortcut key. So a macro named FORMAT would run before a macro named WIDEN. Be sure to use a different shortcut key.

Saving a Macro Sheet

You do not have to do anything special to save the global macro sheet. When you try to exit Excel after recording a macro in the global macro sheet, you'll be prompted to save your changes. Be sure to click OK so that Excel saves your macro in the global macro sheet. It'll automatically be there the next time you start Excel on your computer.

Some Macro Recording Ideas

Here are some macro ideas to ponder as you begin experimenting with Excel's macro recording feature. These suggestions are for creating the kinds of macros you're likely to use every time you work in Excel.

Checklist

▼ Record a macro that applies your favorite combination of formats to any cell in a worksheet. This could include your favorite alignment setting, favorite font typeface and point size, favorite pattern, and favorite number format.

▼ Record a macro that prints multiple copies of a document, one for each department head in your company. (Use the File Print command and specify the number of copies in the Copies text box.)

▼ Record a macro that automatically sorts database records back to their original entry order. Be sure to use the record number column as the first sort key when you're recording.

CHAPTER 18

Excel, Made To Order

IN A NUTSHELL

- ▼ Controlling the look of your worksheets
- ▼ Changing the appearance of the Excel screen
- ▼ Displaying more toolbars
- ▼ Customizing toolbars
- ▼ Attaching a macro to a toolbar

The first hundred hours you spend working in Excel are usually devoted to getting cozy with the program's most-often used features. Once you get by your initial infatuation, certain aspects of working with the program become, well, less exhilarating. When you're ready to put a little spice back into your relationship, you'll be happy to learn that Excel can evolve to suit your changing needs.

You'll see how to add new tools to your screen and how to remove those that you really don't use much. You'll also learn how to control the way data is displayed in your worksheets. When you're finished reading this chapter, you'll be able to forge a new and exciting look for Excel on your computer—a look that's tailored to your own tastes and preferences.

Changing Appearances

(Removing the plain, brown wrapper)

Customizing Excel is a lot like driving in a new car. At first you're happy using just a few basic features, such as adjusting the seat and rear view mirror. The more time you spend with your car, though, the more interested you become in the other amenities, like the side mirrors and the air conditioning vents and the tilt wheel. It's exactly the same with Excel. Once you're comfortable creating, editing, and printing worksheets and charts, you'll want to start tinkering with other things.

Maybe you're a devoted keyboard user who rarely uses a mouse. In that case, remove the toolbar and the scroll bars from your screen. You never use them anyhow. Doing this will free up more screen room for your worksheets. Or try adding a splash of color to your row and column headings. Maybe you'd like to get rid of the gridlines. You can do all of these things and more.

Display It Again, Sam

Open the Options menu and choose the Display command. Excel displays the Display Options dialog box, which is full of lots of interesting check boxes. You can use these settings to control how Excel displays stuff in a worksheet.

The normal settings for the Display Options dialog box

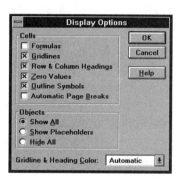

Some of the display options aren't worth learning at this point (or maybe even ever). So let's concentrate only on the ones you can use immediately and will benefit from. Don't be afraid to experiment a little. Nothing will explode.

Learning the really useful display options

▼ Click on the Formulas check box to show formulas instead of their answers in every cell that contains one. This box is normally unchecked, and the feature is therefore turned off. When you turn it on, Excel doubles the size of your worksheet columns so that your formulas have a little more breathing room to reveal themselves. This feature is useful when you want to trace the calculation path of a whole bunch of formulas in the same worksheet (in other words, what numbers affect which formulas and how).

continues

273

Learning the really useful display options, continued

▼ Click on the Gridlines check box to turn off the display of gridlines in a worksheet. This box is normally checked. This display effect is great when you want your worksheet report to look more like a word processing document and less like a worksheet. It's the "anti-worksheet" worksheet setting.

▼ Click on the Row & Column Headings box to remove the row numbers and column letters from your worksheet. This box normally is checked. This feature is another one of those "anti-worksheet" worksheet settings. Try using it in combination with the Gridlines option. Remember, though, that without row and column headings, you won't be able to use the mouse-clicking shortcuts for column width, row height, and the Best Fit feature.

▼ Click on the Zero Values box to turn off the display of zero values. Normally this feature is turned on (the box is checked) so that each time you type a zero value into a cell, the value appears as 0. How convenient! But when you turn it off, any cell that contains a zero, or any formula whose answer is zero, displays as a blank cell. This setting is great for worksheet templates that contain lots of zero values (that is, until someone starts typing in numbers). Warning! Banks, big corporations, and accountants hate to see any financial document that has lots of zeros. Don't worry; Excel will continue to do its math correctly, regardless of whether you can see the zeros.

▼ The Gridline & Heading Color setting actually is a drop-down list. Click on its down arrow to reveal a list of really colorful colors. You can click any of these colors to change the look of your worksheet gridlines and row and column headings. Here's a tip: avoid the color white, because you won't be able to see the letters and numbers.

▼ The other settings are of no use to most Excel users. (But they're great for designing space shuttle warp engines.) Feel free to leave these settings alone and move on to more useful stuff.

This worksheet's gridlines and row and column headings have been removed, and it has been designated a "Show Formulas" zone

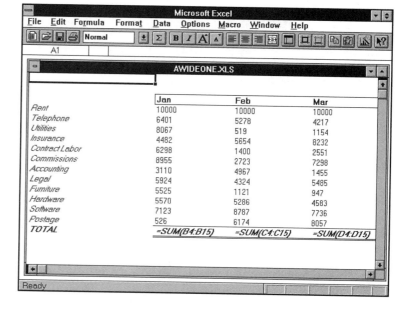

	Microsoft Excel
	File Edit Formula Format Data Options Macro Window Help

A1

AWIDEONE.XLS

	Jan	Feb	Mar
Rent	10000	10000	10000
Telephone	6401	5278	4217
Utilities	8067	519	1154
Insurance	4482	5654	8232
Contract Labor	6298	1400	2551
Commissions	8955	2723	7298
Accounting	3110	4967	1455
Legal	5924	4324	5485
Furniture	5525	1121	947
Hardware	5570	5286	4583
Software	7123	8787	7736
Postage	526	6174	8057
TOTAL	=SUM(B4:B15)	=SUM(C4:C15)	=SUM(D4:D15)

Ready

"I HATE THIS!"

I changed the settings, but my new worksheet is back to the ugly, old style!

The settings you choose in the Display Options dialog box affect only the current worksheet, even if you have more than one worksheet open. You have to adjust each worksheet individually. When you save the worksheet, the settings are saved for the next time you work with that worksheet.

Settings that affect all worksheets are in the Workspace Options dialog box, coming up in the next section.

Decorating Your Workspace

Had enough of the display options? Then try Excel's workspace options. Open the Options menu and choose the Workspace command. When Excel displays the Workspace Options dialog box, you'll be struck by how similar it looks to the Display Options dialog box. Lots and lots of little check boxes. Don't worry if your dialog box looks different. Anything that's been checked can be unchecked. Really, I've checked.

The normal settings for the Workspace Options dialog box

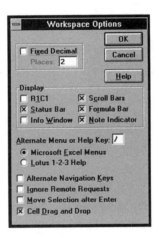

Have you noticed that some of the workspace settings seem like they belong in the Display Options dialog box? Like that block in the middle that's labeled "Display"? A common first impression. The workspace options are different simply because they affect every worksheet—even the ones you haven't even opened yet. In fact, what these settings really control is the look and feel of Excel's workspace.

I HATE EXCEL!

BUZZWORDS

WORKSPACE

The word "workspace"—you may or may not care to know—refers to the area where Excel displays its worksheets. The Workspace Options dialog box settings control not only where the stuff on your worksheet is displayed, but also how certain things work inside your worksheet. (Hey, I don't make these rules up; I just ignore them.)

As with any dialog box that looks like a presidential election ballot, only some of the candidates are worthy of your consideration. Let's concentrate on the ones that hold the best hope for the future (of your worksheet, that is). And don't be afraid to experiment a little. Nothing will explode, and impeachment is always an option.

Learning the really useful workspace options

▼ Click on the Fixed Decimal box to select where you want the decimal point to appear in your worksheet numbers. By clicking on this box and then typing a value in the Places box, you can increase or decrease the precision of decimal values in your worksheet. This setting normally is turned off (unchecked). Whenever you type a decimal number, Excel places the decimal where you want it, but by setting this option to 2, for instance, any number you type *without* a decimal will show a decimal point two digits to the left. Excel would therefore display the number 456 as 4.56 and the number 21 as 0.21. This feature is helpful when you're using your numeric keypad to type lots of currency numbers and would prefer not to have to type that darn decimal point again and again and again.

continues

▼ Click on the Status Bar box to remove the status bar from your screen. This setting normally is turned on so that you can see Excel's status messages on the status bar. Turn it off when you could care less about anything that Excel has to say.

▼ Click on the Scroll Bars box to remove the horizontal and vertical scroll bars from your screen. This setting normally is turned on so that you can see the scroll bars. All you mouse haters will benefit from the extra screen space you get when you turn off this feature.

▼ Click on the Formula Bar box to remove the formula bar from your screen. This setting normally is turned on so that you can see the formula bar and watch as you type stuff into your worksheet. Turn it off when you get really cocky and feel like working blindfolded in Excel.

▼ Click on the Move Selection After Enter box so that Excel automatically advances the active cell down one row each time you press Enter or click on the Enter box to complete a cell entry. Also known in worksheet circles as "Excel's Little Helper," this feature normally is turned off.

▼ Click on the Cell Drag and Drop option to turn this feature off. Once off, you will no longer be able to drag and drop things in your worksheet. (What a drag!) But don't do it, because it's one of the coolest and most useful features around. Go back and reread Chapter 9 if you don't believe me.

I HATE EXCEL!

Hanging Out in Your Favorite Toolbar

Throughout this book you've been looking at figures that show a single toolbar at the top of the screen. It's called the "Standard toolbar," and by now it has probably become your close personal friend. But the Standard toolbar is by no means an only child. In fact, it comes from a rather large and talented family of Excel productivity tools.

The Toolbar Family

To visit the toolbar family, open the Options menu and choose the Toolbars command. Excel shows you the Toolbars dialog box. It's where the toolbar family lives. All nine of them.

There are nine different toolbars in Excel

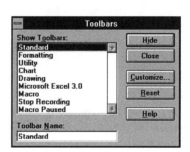

Each toolbar's name (for the most part) describes what it does. Do you want to look at one more closely? Click on its name in the Show Toolbars list; then click on the Show button. Excel pops the toolbar onto your screen, between the Standard toolbar and the formula bar. You can continue adding other toolbars this same way.

▼ The Formatting toolbar groups together some useful formatting tools. There are two drop-down lists that let you quickly change the current font and point size; three number formatting tools; two tools that increase and decrease the number of decimal places in a number; a tool that adds light shading to a cell; and others.

▼ The Utility toolbar provides an interesting combination of editing, rearranging, and viewing tools. The first two tools undo and repeat worksheet actions; the next three tools copy a worksheet selection and then let you paste either values or formats; there are tools for zooming your worksheet view in and out, tools for sorting selected rows in ascending and descending order, and more.

▼ The Chart toolbar is explicitly devoted to helping you chart worksheet numbers. With these tools, you can choose a chart category; embed a chart in a worksheet; edit the current chart with ChartWizard; and add or delete a legend.

▼ The Drawing toolbar contains tools that help you draw graphic images in your worksheet or chart. These tools draw lines, arrows, squiggly lines, transparent geometric shapes, and filled geometric shapes, and they also let you edit the shape or color of any embedded object.

▼ The Microsoft Excel 3.0 toolbar is exactly what it sounds like. It's the toolbar that originally came with Microsoft Excel 3.0. If you never used that version of this program, you can ignore this one. If you've just upgraded from version 3.0, however, you can ease the transition by showing this toolbar on your screen.

▼ The Macro toolbar is dedicated to helping you manage your macros. Among other things, this toolbar's tools can open a new macro sheet, record a new macro, run a macro, and stop a macro from running.

TIP

Here's the best way to figure out which tool does what. Place your mouse pointer on the tool that's making you curious, click and hold down the left mouse button, and then read the tool's description in the status bar. When you're finished reading, drag your mouse pointer away from the tool BEFORE you release the mouse button. As long as you follow these steps precisely, you can figure out what each tool does without actually having to use it.

Organizing Your Toolbars

There's lots of stuff you can do with toolbars besides displaying them on-screen. One thing you can do is move them around Excel's workspace by dragging and dropping them. When you drop a toolbar in the middle of a worksheet, it actually floats there in space. You want to get rid of a toolbar that's floating in your worksheet? Click on that tiny little Close icon in the top left corner of the toolbar.

Checklist

▼ To float a toolbar in the active worksheet window, click anywhere on the outer perimeter of the toolbar; then drag it and drop it. You also can double-click between any two tools in the toolbar; Excel will immediately float it in your worksheet.

▼ To move a floating toolbar back on top of the formula bar, drag it there and drop it. Excel will do its best to make the toolbar fit correctly. You also can double-click between any two tools in the toolbar, and Excel will immediately reposition the toolbar above the formula bar.

continues

Checklist, continued

▼ A floating toolbar actually sits in its own window, just like a worksheet sits in its own window. You can resize a floating toolbar by dragging its window border in the direction you want to size it. This makes for some interesting-looking toolbars.

▼ Every toolbar has a shortcut menu. You can display this menu by pointing at a toolbar and right-clicking your mouse. From the shortcut menu, you can display another toolbar by clicking on its name in the list. Excel places a check mark by the toolbar name and displays the toolbar on your screen.

▼ Click on Toolbar near the bottom of the shortcut menu to display the Toolbar dialog box. This is the same dialog box you get when you choose the Options Toolbar command.

▼ There are three ways to remove a toolbar from your screen: one, click on its Close icon (top left corner) if the toolbar is floating in your worksheet; two, uncheck its name on any toolbar shortcut menu; and three, select its name in the Toolbars dialog box and then click on the Hide button.

Microsoft Excel

File Edit Formula Format Data Options Macro Window Help

Normal | MS Sans Serif | 10 | **B** *I* U K | $ % , | | |

Normal | Σ B I A A | | | |

A1

BRADY.XLS

	A	B	C	D	E	F	G	H	I
1									
2			The Brady Bunch						
3			Cast Member Favorability Ratings (1 to 10 Scale)						
4									
5			*1973*	*1974*	*1975*	*1976*	*1977*		
6		Mike		2	4	7	5		
7		Carol		0	5	8	5		
8		Greg		0	3	7	10		
9		Marcia	8	0	2	8	10		
10		Jan		2	7	8	4		
11		Peter	8	0	7	9	8		
12		Bobby		0	6	9	7		
13		Cindy		0	9	10	6		
14		Alice	8	2	10	10	6		
15									
16		AVERAGE:	8.0	0.7	5.9	8.4	6.8		

Utility

Macro

Ready

Floating toolbars arranged so that you can see the worksheet in the background

Making Additions to the Toolbar Family

Like Excel, toolbars can be changed to suit your every whim and fancy. The nine members of Excel's toolbar family are Microsoft's "ideal" combination of tools. But what if you prefer using different combinations for your own work? Maybe you'd like to knock a few tools off the Formatting toolbar, and then add on a couple of other tools? It's easy enough to do. Just customize it.

Here's how you can add a tool to a toolbar:

1. Display the toolbar you want to customize.

2. Open the Options menu, choose the Toolbars command, and click on the Customize button. Or, open the shortcut menu for the toolbar you're going to customize; then click on the Customize option.

Excel displays the Customize dialog box.

3. Click on the category name that describes the tool you want to add. The categories are organized pretty much by task. The File category offers tools that do stuff with your files, the Edit category shows you the editing tools, and so on.

4. In the Tools list, locate the tool you want to add. If you're not sure what a particular tool does, click on it to display a brief description at the bottom of the dialog box.

5. Drag the tool out of the Customize dialog box, move it on top of the toolbar you're customizing, and drop it there. You might have to reposition your Customize dialog box to do this.

6. Click on the Close button to return to your worksheet.

That's it! You've just added a tool to a toolbar. Could it be any easier? I think not.

Other ways to customize toolbars

▼ To delete a tool from any toolbar, display the Customize dialog box; then drag the tool off the toolbar and drop it into your worksheet. It'll disappear into thin air, and Excel will quickly reorganize your toolbar to fill in the missing space. Simple.

▼ To return any built-in toolbar to its original state, click on its name in the Toolbars dialog box and click on the Reset button. Any customization you've done to that toolbar is eliminated.

▼ To create a completely original toolbar, open the Toolbars dialog box, type a new name inside the Toolbar Name box, and click on the Add button. Excel immediately displays the Customize dialog box and adds an empty toolbar to your screen. The name you chose appears at the top of the empty toolbar. Add any tools you want; then click on the Close button to return to your worksheet.

▼ To shuffle the order of tools on a toolbar, open the Customize dialog box and then drag and drop the tools to their new pecking order.

▼ To copy a tool from one toolbar to another, display the Customize dialog box, press and hold down the Ctrl key, click on the tool you want to copy, drag it to the destination toolbar, and then drop it. You can use this trick only while the Customize dialog box is open.

▼ To delete a custom toolbar, click on its name in the Toolbars dialog box and click on the Delete button. When Excel asks whether you're sure that you want to delete the toolbar. Click OK if you are.

▼ Excel won't let you delete any of its built-in toolbars. After all, they are family.

EXPERTS ONLY

Attaching a macro to a tool on the toolbar

The last category of tools in the Customize dialog box is called Custom. The tools in this category are fairly generic: they have icons, but no specific purpose attached to them. Excel allows you to attach a macro to any of these generic tools and then add the tool to any toolbar. That way, when you click on the tool, your macro will run. Here's how to do it.

I HATE EXCEL!

EXPERTS ONLY

As soon as you drag a custom tool (one that you created) onto a toolbar, Excel displays the Assign To Tool dialog box. This dialog box contains the names of all the macros that exist in Excel's global macro sheet. If you also happen to have a macro sheet, that sheet's macros also appear on this list. Click on the macro name you want to attach to the tool; then click OK. When Excel returns you to the Customize dialog box, click on the Close button to return to your worksheet. Now click on the custom tool and watch as Excel runs the macro you attached to it.

Suppose, though, that you didn't actually have a macro ready to attach to a custom tool. No problem. In the Assign To Tool dialog box, just click on the Record button. When the Record Macro dialog box appears, type the name of the macro and the shortcut key. Choose OK. Excel begins recording the macro. When you're finished recording, click on the Stop tool that Excel conveniently displays in the worksheet. As soon as you do, Excel attaches the macro to your custom tool. (Wow! Is this awesome or what?!) Now try running the macro by clicking on the tool.

PART VI

Quick & Dirty Dozens

I HATE EXCEL

Quick & Dirty Dozens

IN A NUTSHELL

- ▼ 12 cool things nobody knows you can do with Excel
- ▼ 12 things you should never do in Excel
- ▼ 12 heart-stopping messages and what to do about them
- ▼ 12 most common mistakes
- ▼ 12 best Excel shortcuts
- ▼ 12 features you can monkey with if you have time to kill

12 Cool Things Nobody Knows You Can Do with Excel

1. **Stashing your favorite worksheets, charts, and macros**

So you have a favorite worksheet that you like to work on, first thing every morning? What? You have a favorite macro sheet, too? Then go ahead and tell Excel to fire up those documents each time you start the program on your computer. That way you don't have to select the File Open command over and over and over again.

Here's how: Save the documents you want to use at start-up time in the XLSTART subdirectory. This subdirectory is just under the directory that contains Excel's important files—usually called EXCEL or EXCEL4 or something close to that. Each time you start Excel on your computer, the program looks in XLSTART for your favorite worksheets, charts, and macros. If none are there, Excel displays the blank worksheet called SHEET1. When Excel does find documents in XLSTART, it displays them as soon as Excel starts on your computer.

2. **Finding things when you don't know what you're looking for**

The Find and Replace commands on the Formula menu are cool for helping you quickly locate and change things in large worksheets. The basic premise of this feature is that you know what you're looking for and what you want to replace it with. Fortunately, you're in luck when you're not exactly sure what you're looking for but you do have some clue.

Suppose that you've been asked to search for every occurrence of a word. You've searched through the worksheet several times, but Excel can't find any matches. You know the word's there and you suspect that you've misspelled it. Here's what to do.

Choose the Formula Replace command. In the Find box, type as much of the word as you know to be correct; then use a wild-card symbol for the rest. For instance, the entry **TOT*** will find *Total*, *Totals*, and *Totally*. The entry ***MBER** finds the words *December*, *November*, and *September*. The entry **???Q** finds all entries that have four characters (including spaces) and end in the letter *Q*. So it finds stuff like *1st Q*, *2nd Q*, *3rd Q*, and *4th Q*.

3. **I need more decimals, please**

When you format your numbers using the Number, Currency, and Percentage formats, Excel displays your numbers with either two or no decimal places. There are no other choices. So what happens when you need to display more decimal places?

Open the Format menu and choose the Number command. In the Number Format dialog box, choose the format you want to use. They appear in the Category list. Before you click OK to apply the format, click inside the Code box, where Excel displays the code you're about to apply. At the end of the current code entry, type the numbers of extra decimal places you want to show.

For example, to change the code **#,##0.00** so that it shows three decimal places, type an extra zero to make it look like this: **#,##0.000**. Now click OK to apply the format. Or, to change the code **0.00%** so that it displays only one decimal place, delete one of the zeros: **0.0%**.

4. **Stopping prying hands from changing things**

Protect your Excel worksheets by safeguarding them against prying hands and fumbling fingers. Every office has at least one pair of these. You know, the snooping coworker who loves to tinker around on your computer while you're away at lunch. It's important that these busybodies be prevented from changing things in worksheets you leave open on-screen.

First, open a worksheet and select the cell range you want to protect. Now open the Format menu and choose the Cell Protection command. Inside the Cell Protection dialog box, verify that the Locked check box is checked. If it isn't, be sure to click on it before you continue. Click OK to return to your worksheet.

Next, open the Options menu and choose the Protect Document command. In the dialog box that appears, make sure that these check boxes are checked: Cells, Objects, and Windows. In the Password text box type the password you want to assign to your worksheet. Pick something easy so that you'll remember it. Now click OK. When you're prompted to verify the password, retype it exactly as before. Click OK to return to your worksheet.

Now, anytime someone tries to change anything in your worksheet, or close it with the File Close command, or even move the worksheet window, that person will be stopped by a message that says, "Locked cells cannot be changed."

To unprotect your document later so you can use it, open the Options menu and choose the Unprotect command. (It's in exactly the same spot in the menu as the Protect Document command was.) In the Document Password dialog box, type the password and click OK to regain control of your worksheet.

5. Preventing prying eyes from stealing a peek

Guarding worksheets from prying hands and fumbling fingers offers no protection against prying eyes—and we know that every office has lots of these. You see, some Excel worksheet information is so private that you'll be forced to swallow your computer whole, lest your Excel files fall into the hands of industrial spies. When your stomach just isn't up to that particular challenge, you can instead assign a password that controls who may open and work with the worksheets stored on your computer's hard drive.

Open the worksheet you want to protect with a password. Open the File menu and choose the Save As command. Click on the Options button in the Save As dialog box. In the Save Options dialog box, type a password into the Protection Password box; then click OK. You'll be asked to confirm the password by typing it again. After you retype it, click OK to save your worksheet with its new password. The next time you (or someone else) attempt to open the worksheet on your computer, you have to type the correct password before Excel will open it.

BEWARE: Don't forget your password because without it, you cannot open up your worksheet. Ever. Without exception.

6. **Juggling several worksheets at once**

Whenever you have two or more worksheets open at the same time, it's easy to move information between them by using the Edit Copy and Edit Paste commands. Suppose that you have two worksheets open on-screen—let's call them Worksheet 1 and Worksheet 2. You start by copying any cell range in Worksheet 1. When you're finished, click your mouse inside Worksheet 2 to activate its window. Once inside Worksheet 2, click on the cell where you want to place the copy; then choose the Edit Paste command. Voilà! Your information appears in Worksheet 2 exactly as is did in Worksheet 1.

Stay alert when the range you're copying contains formulas. When you copy formulas from Worksheet 1 to Worksheet 2, be sure to bring along all the original numbers that the formulas use in the Worksheet 1 calculations. When you do this, Excel will be able to adjust your relative reference formulas correctly, regardless of where you choose to paste the information in Worksheet 2.

When you copy absolute reference formulas, those formulas will calculate whatever is inside the same range on the other

worksheet. Suppose that you copy the formula **SUM($A$1:$A$5)** from Worksheet 1 to Worksheet 2. When the formula is pasted into Worksheet 2, the formula will not change one bit. The answer that the copied formula displays in Worksheet 2 depends entirely on whatever numbers happen to be in cell range A1:A5 in Worksheet 2.

7. Range names you can sink your teeth into

Name a range and suddenly you have a powerful thing at your fingertips. I'm not talking about cell names, either, which sound like stars from distant galaxies. You know the type, names like H1450 or IV397. I'm talking about plain-English names that not only make sense to you and me, but make sense to every stranger who might meander into your worksheet one day. Fact is, names like BOB and GOOBER5 are easier (and much more fun) to remember than cell F5 or cell range G6..P23.

To name a cell, or a range of cells, open the Formula menu and choose the Define Name command. In the dialog box that opens, notice that your cell address or cell range appears in the Refers To box. All that's left to do is name the range. Hmmm. How about Ashley? No, too yuppie-ish. How about Vincent? No, too dark. How about Madonna? Blechhh! I've got it, let's use SALES93 since it's the range that contains the 1993 sales data. Type **SALES93** into the Refers To box and click OK. You've just named your first range.

Now that you've named it, what do you do with it? Good question. Suppose that you need to add all the numbers in that range. Try this function on for size: **=SUM(SALES93)**. Or maybe you need to reformat the values in the range that contains the 1993 sales data. You're down around row 9,000 and your fingers are getting tired from pressing PgDn and PgUp to move around. Here's a faster method. Press F5, click on the name SALES93 in the list, and click OK. Excel moves you there pronto. Format away!

8. Insert a painting into a worksheet

You already know that a chart is one type of object you can embed into a Excel worksheet, but there are lots of other types of objects you can embed. For instance, you can embed objects that were created in other programs. Let's check out how to do this with the Paintbrush program, since everyone who owns Windows also owns this little beauty.

Open the Edit menu and choose the Insert Object command. Excel displays the Insert Object dialog box. Click on the Paintbrush Picture option in the Object Type list; then click OK. Excel immediately draws a blank object in your worksheet; the object is surrounded by edit handles.

But something else also happens. Excel starts the Paintbrush program and pops it onto your screen right on top of your newly embedded object and your worksheet window. At this point you can create a new picture in the Paintbrush window. (If you don't know how to use Paintbrush, check out its built-in Help system. It works just like the one in Excel.) Once you're done creating, open Paintbrush's File menu and choose the Exit & Return To command. Paintbrush will ask whether you want to update the open embedded object before continuing. Click OK to signal that you do. Paintbrush closes, and you're sent back into Excel. The picture you created now appears inside the embedded object in your worksheet. You can drag and resize the Paintbrush object the same way you do with embedded chart objects.

What an artist you are!

9. Checking your spelling in a worksheet

What? A spreadsheet program that can check the spelling of the words in my worksheet? No way. Amazing, but true!

To "spell check" your worksheet, click on the Select All button (it's the blank button at the area where the row heading and column heading meet). Then open the Options menu and choose the Spelling command. Excel displays the Spelling dialog box. The first entry it encounters that it doesn't recognize appears in the Change To box. Type in your correction here, or click the correctly spelled version of the word in the Suggestions list; then click the Change button. Excel corrects the misspelled word and continues checking for other misspelled words.

In worksheets, it's common to use abbreviated words like JAN for January or AVE for average. Excel always stops at these kinds of words because it thinks that you misspelled them. Click on the Ignore All button to move past every occurrence of such a word. Excel will continue checking your worksheet. When it's finished checking the entire worksheet, Excel displays the message `Finished spelling entire sheet`. Click OK to move back to your worksheet.

Be sure to save all the spelling corrections in your worksheet. Use the File Save command.

10. **Toolbars to the right, toolbars to the left**

Toolbars normally appear at the top of your worksheet, between the formula bar and the menu bar. You can position a toolbar in other parts of a worksheet window, such as just above the status bar or at the left or right side of the worksheet. Any area in your Excel screen that accepts a toolbar is called a *toolbar dock*.

To dock a toolbar, drag it to the location where you want to show it, and release your mouse. If you drag the Standard toolbar down the screen and release it near the status bar, Excel will dock it there. If you drag the Chart toolbar to the right edge of your screen and release it, Excel will dock it there.

The only limitation to docking is that Excel won't let you dock any toolbar that contains a list box (like the Standard and Formatting toolbars) at either the right or left side of the window.

11. **Editing two worksheets for the price of one**

So you have twelve worksheets that you need to edit? And each worksheet was created from the same template, right? You're asking yourself why there isn't an easier way to edit a group of worksheets that all look exactly the same. Hey, there is!

Open all the worksheets you want to edit. Next, open the Options menu and choose the Group Edit command. In the Group Edit dialog box, click on the name of the first worksheet you want to edit; then hold down the Ctrl key and click on the names of all the other ones you want to edit. Now click OK. Excel returns you to the first worksheet in the group. Notice that the phrase [Group] appears in each worksheet's title bar. This lets you know which worksheets are part of the group you're editing in group mode.

Now, before you do anything else, listen to this. From this point on, anything you do to the *active* worksheet is also done to every other worksheet in the group. If you type the number 500 into cell F5, that same number is entered into cell F5 of all the other worksheets. Change the width of column D in the active worksheet, and that same column width changes in every other worksheet. While in group mode, anything you do to the active worksheet by using the File, Edit, and Format menu commands gets done to every worksheet in the group. Absolutely cool, huh?

When you're finished making all your changes, you can end group mode by clicking inside any other worksheet that's part of the group. You also can select another worksheet's name from the Window menu to end group mode, but before you do this, be sure to choose the File Save command so that you can simultaneously save every worksheet that's open!

12. Unfilling filled ranges

Do you know how easy it is to fill in a cell range with sequential numbers or with words? Type a number (like 100) or a word (like JAN) into a cell. Then click on that cell to make it active. Now drag that cell's fill handle to the last cell in the range, and then release.

Well, suppose you decide that you don't need all 6,000 of the numbers you just filled into the cell range. Suppose that you need only 4,000 of them. You can unfill any cell range that you just filled simply by dragging the cell's fill handle backward through the range you just filled. When you drag backward through a fill range, Excel temporarily shades the cells you're unfilling so you know exactly where you are at all times. As soon as you release the mouse, all the shaded cells disappear, as if you never filled them in the first place.

12 Things You Should Never Do in Excel

1. Never delete files you don't recognize

Feel free to use the File Delete command to delete worksheets, macro sheets, and charts you don't need any more. These kinds of documents usually end in XLS, XLM, or XLC. But don't ever delete a file you don't recognize, even if it has one of these familiar file endings.

At all costs, avoid deleting any files from the EXCEL directory. That's where Excel keeps the files it needs in order to run. These files have endings like DLL, EXE, HLP, XLM, and REG. If you delete one of them, you'd better run … and hide.

2. Never close a worksheet without saving it

I know, it seems unlikely, but the fact is that lots of Excel users have closed worksheets without saving them, only to regret the decision later on.

Excel never forgets. It's the elephant of the software kingdom. When Excel asks whether you want to save changes to a worksheet, you better do just that, even if you don't need the changes. That way the worst thing that could possibly happen is that you'll have a useless worksheet saved on your hard disk. Feel free to get rid of it later on, when you've got your wits about you again.

3. Never start typing without knowing where you are

Some people get so quick with the keyboard that they can type for long periods of time without needing to glance at the screen. But Excel doesn't warn you when you are typing over something else.

Stay aware of where you are in your Excel worksheet, because all it takes is one slip of the hand. You accidentally hit the PgUp key without knowing it. Excel sends you flying back up the page with nary a chirp or click to let you know what's about to happen. So you keep pounding away on your keyboard, unaware that you're typing over all the stuff at the top of your worksheet. It's a bummer—believe me, I know.

4. **Never run a macro while the macro sheet is active**

Don't run a macro while its macro sheet is showing on-screen. Always be sure that your worksheet is active before you run a macro.

Many a recorded macro has gone down the tubes simply because the macro sheet—instead of a worksheet—was active when the macro was started. It usually happens after you've been working long and hard to record a macro. You're excited because you're eager to test it immediately. You hit that macro shortcut key, look up at your screen, and freeze in shock as you watch the macro munch itself. Rows are deleting everywhere, whole cell ranges are being cut and pasted. Suddenly everything screeches to a halt. Most of what's left on your screen is unrecognizable. You press Ctrl+Z in hopes of undoing all this mayhem, but Excel only brings back the very last row it deleted. You swear you'll never record a macro again.

5. **Never start two copies of Excel on your computer**

Program Manager is one of the coolest things about Windows. It has all those little icons that make it so simple to start programs. In fact, with Excel running on your computer, you can switch back to Program Manager to start a different program. Maybe Word, for instance.

Some Excel users switch to Program Manager before they leave for lunch. Suppose that you are one of those users. You come back to your desk an hour later and double-click on the Excel icon in Program Manager. Windows starts a second copy of the program on your computer. This gets even more complicated when you try to open the worksheet you were using before, the one that currently is active in the other copy of Excel that's running on your computer. This is confusing, isn't it? That's why you should always avoid starting two copies of Excel on your computer. But when you've already done it, the best way to proceed is to exit the most recent copy of the program and then switch back to the other one.

6. Never group edit worksheets that look different

The group editing feature saves you tons of time when you have several worksheets that use the exact same design layout, such as a multi-divisional company might use to report its monthly financial data, using four separate—but identically constructed—worksheets.

Don't use this feature, though, to edit a group of worksheets that have nothing to do with one another. Just because one worksheet looks great with column C widened to 15 doesn't means that every other worksheet you create will. Here's an even scarier prospect. Suppose that you delete column C from the active worksheet. Excel immediately deletes the same column from every other worksheet you've selected for group editing. But what's the likelihood that four unrelated worksheets all need to have column C deleted? "Ooops!" is right.

7. Never use spaces to align stuff in cells

Don't use the space bar to align stuff in your cells. It's tempting to do this, especially if you developed the bad habit from years of using word processing programs. When you use the space bar to align words and numbers in cells, things might look lined up on-screen,

but they rarely appear lined up when you print the worksheet onto paper. Use the alignment tools in the Standard toolbar instead. For even more alignment options, use the Alignment command on the Format menu.

8. **Never forget your passwords**

A forgotten password is a sure ticket to the unemployment line—or at least to the corner of your office with a dunce hat. Without the correct password, you have absolutely no way to get that worksheet open. Call every computer nerd you know, and they'll all say the same thing: "Didn't you write down the password somewhere?"

If you use passwords to protect your worksheets, write them down somewhere. Scribble them on a piece of paper and mail them to your aunt in New Delhi for safekeeping. Better yet, get a safe-deposit box at a bank in Switzerland. Whatever you do, don't rely on your memory. You just never know when you might get a bump on your head going to work one day.

9. **Never open files you don't recognize into Excel**

Here's the counterpart to the warning about deleting files you don't recognize. Don't open a file into Excel if you don't recognize it. The only files you should be working with end in XLS, XLC, or XLM. Everything else is off-limits.

You see, Excel is good about trying to recognize any file you instruct it to open. That's because the program is designed to use certain files that were created with other programs. But we don't care about those other programs right now. Where you'll get into trouble is when you do open a non-Excel file, enter or change a bit of data, and then do something innocent like saving the file. (Heck, you've already been warned to save your files as much as possible.) You'll permanently ruin files or make other software programs on your computer unusable if you do this. So don't!

10. **Never sort the field names into your database**

Always leave the field names row out of your range selection when you're sorting a database. If you don't, Excel will sort the field names row into your database as if it were just another record. When this happens, the Data Form command won't work properly. And that, after all, is the #1 coolest way of doing that database thing in Excel.

11. **Never transpose a cell range onto itself**

So you've got a topsy-turvy worksheet and you want to make it look right. Well go do it somewhere else, will ya? Hey, no kidding. When you paste a cell range with the Paste Special command's Transpose option turned on, don't paste the range onto itself. You might screw things up. Instead, paste the transposed range into a blank area of the worksheet. That way you can compare the transposed data to the original data and see whether it's exactly what you wanted. Only then should you consider moving the transposed cell range back on top of the original cell range.

12. **Never forget to save, save again, and then save once more just to be sure**

Every Excel user who's lazy about saving worksheets eventually resorts to the "fish story" excuse. That's where you claim to have finished a piece of work, but your claim can't be independently verified by an unimpeachable source. In other words, you were working on the fiscal-year-end financial report, when all of a sudden the electricity went off, or some bozo put a knee into your computer's Reset button, or the mail clerk walked by and tripped over your power cord.

Bottom line: your work is gone forever, and there's no way in hell your boss is going to believe that you really did the work. Moral to the story? Save often and as if your life depended on it.

12 Heart-Stopping Messages and What To Do about Them

1. General Protection Fault

The "General Protection Fault" message is the one message you hope you never see. It means that something has gone seriously wrong in Windows or in Excel, and Windows can't really do anything about it. Most of the time, this message displays an OK button, an Ignore button, and a some other meaningless gibberish.

Start by clicking on the Ignore button. You might have to do this several times before anything happens. If Excel miraculously comes back to life, immediately save all your work, exit Excel, and exit Windows.

When clicking on Ignore has no effect, you must click OK. Windows probably will exit Excel, and you will lose any unsaved worksheets. At this point, it's best to exit Windows and start all over again. If clicking OK has no effect, press the Reset button on the front of your computer, or press Ctrl+Alt+Del to restart your computer.

2. Insufficient memory to run this application.
Quit one or more Windows applications and then try again.

When you see this message, Windows is telling you that you have so many other programs running on your computer that there's no room left to run Excel. Click OK to get rid of this message box. Exit as many of the other programs as you can; then try again.

If closing other programs still doesn't seem to work, try exiting and restarting Windows. This time, be sure that Excel is the first (and only) program you run when you get to the Program Manager window.

3. **Document is being modified by [*name*]. Open as Read-Only?**

This error message can give you the creeps; it's not only heart-stopping, but it displays the name of someone you know in the spot marked [*name*]. This message usually appears when you're running Excel from a network and are trying to open a worksheet. Here are the two possible problems.

One possibility is that you're trying to open a worksheet that some-one else on your network is using at the moment. If you can wait a while, click No and try opening it later. If you need it immediately, click No, go find that person and tell him or her to get out of your worksheet, and then try again. If you only need to review the infor-mation in the worksheet, click OK. This allows you to look at the worksheet, but you won't be allowed to save it.

The other possibility is that when this message appears, the name in the box is yours. (Talk about really creepy!) In this case you've probably opened a second copy of Excel on your computer, and you're trying to open the same worksheet that's already open in the first copy of Excel. Exit the second copy of Excel; then switch to the first copy. Your worksheet will be there.

4. **[*filename*] was created in a previous version of Microsoft Excel. Do you want to update it to Microsoft Excel 4.0 format?**

This message isn't quite as serious at it sounds. You're trying to save a worksheet that originally was created in Excel 3.0. If you need to keep the file in a format that Excel 3.0 can use, click No. Next, choose the File Save As command. In the Save As dialog box, choose Excel 3.0 from the Save File as Type list, type your name in the File Name box, and then click OK.

If you don't need to keep the file in the Excel 3.0 format, click Yes. Excel saves it in the Excel 4.0 format, and you'll never get this message again—not from this file, anyway.

5. **Drive does not exist/Path does not exist/Cannot find this file**

These three messages are essentially saying the same thing. Excel doesn't recognize the disk drive, the path name, or the worksheet name you typed into the Open dialog box. Check to be sure that you've spelled everything correctly and that the worksheet you're trying to open really is located there. Click OK to try again.

6. **Cannot do that command on a multiple selection**

Excel is really great about letting you do things to disconnected ranges of cells. You can format them, erase their contents, and even copy them. Some things you try to do to disconnected cell ranges cause Excel to go berserk, like trying to cut and paste a disconnected range of cells. You can't. Excel won't let you. So stop trying, and you'll never see this message again. Instead, cut and paste things one cell range at a time.

7. **Cannot quit Microsoft Excel**

Just like the little pink bunny in the commercial, Excel sometimes refuses to quit. It just keeps going and going and going. This error message usually appears right after you press Alt+F4 to quit the program. (In case you forgot, that's the shortcut key for the File Exit command.)

If Excel is still in the middle of doing something, like calculating a complex formula or running a macro, it won't let you exit. Occasionally you'll get this message when you press Alt+F4 while a dialog box is still on-screen. In any case, be sure to let Excel finish what it's doing before you try to quit again.

8. **Cannot save to an open document**

This message appears whenever you attempt to save a worksheet using the name of another worksheet that's already open in Excel.

Suppose that you choose the Save As command from the File menu and, in the Save As dialog box, click on the name of a file in the File Name list. Then, when you click OK, the error message appears. What do you do?

Cancel the Save As command by clicking on the Cancel button. Now open the Window menu and click on the name of the worksheet that's causing the problem. Close it with the Close command. Now, if you really want to save the other worksheet using the closed worksheet's name, choose the Save As command again.

9. Disk is full

This message crops up for lots of different reasons. Here are the most common ones.

Your hard disk has run out of storage room. The worksheet you're trying to save will not fit. Delete some files from your hard disk and try saving again. If you don't normally delete files, or if you aren't sure which ones you can delete, try saving your worksheet to a floppy disk.

If you got the error message just after you tried saving to a floppy disk, pull the disk out of its drive and see whether it has been write-protected. For 5 1/4-inch disks, there'll be a little piece of plastic tape about an inch from the top right edge of your disk. Remove it. If you're using 3 1/2-inch disks, flip your disk over to the side where there's a little black push-tab in the top left corner of the disk. Slide this tab down. Now try again.

If you still get this error message, or if you're sure that your floppy disk is not write-protected, you'll have to delete some files from your floppy before you can save the worksheet there.

If all else fails, go get a blank, formatted floppy disk.

10. Incorrect password

Ooops! You typed in your password incorrectly. Open the File menu, choose the Open command, and try again. If you still can't get it open, go call that aunt in New Delhi who has a copy of your passwords. Or was it a safe-deposit box in your Swiss bank?

What, you never wrote down your password anywhere? Better luck next time. Your worksheet is gone. Forever. As in never to be recovered unless you can remember your password. Can you say, "I Hate Excel"?

11. Not enough memory. Continue without Undo?

Yes, this message indicates that Excel is getting on in years. It can't quite remember things like it used to. So be careful, because if you click OK (which means that you've decided to go ahead with whatever it was you were doing before this message appeared), Excel will not be able to undo it. So if you choose Edit Undo or press Ctrl+Z, nothing will happen. Those twelve rows you accidentally deleted will remain deleted. If you'd rather not take any chances, click on Cancel to get back to your worksheet. Then save the worksheet and exit Excel. Start up Excel again, open the worksheet, and try doing that operation over.

12. Overwrite non-blank cells in destination?

I know this message is a drag, but that's what got you into trouble in the first place. You dragged a cell range to a new location in your worksheet, and that new location has stuff in it. If you click on Yes, Excel will move the dragged range on top of the other range, thereby overwriting the other range. Think about this before you do it. Click on Cancel to save yourself from making a terrible mistake. (Even if you accidentally overwrite the other cell range, you always can press Ctrl+Z to undo the mistake.)

12 Most Common Mistakes

1. **Excel won't start when I double-click on its icon**

The most common complaint about Windows is that it's hard to double-click icons fast enough to get a program started. Double-clicking a mouse button definitely is an acquired skill. You might have to practice this stroke a few billion times before you get it right.

Here's an easier way to start Excel. In Program Manager, click on the Excel icon once to highlight it; then press Enter to start the program.

2. **Sometimes when I type, Excel beeps and flashes stuff**

You're typing along merrily when all of a sudden your computer beeps at you, flashes a menu, or shows some error message that has nothing to do with what you were typing. So you hit Esc a few times and start typing again—everything is fine. What happened? You inadvertently hit the Alt key while you were typing.

The Alt key is located to the left (and sometimes also to the right) of the space bar key. Pressing the Alt key activates Excel's menu bar. Normally, if you were accessing the menu bar this way, you'd press a single key to open one of Excel's menus. But if you don't realize that you pressed the Alt key, you'll just keep typing along. Excel's reaction to all this typing depends on which keys you happen to press next.

If the first key you hit happens to be one of the keys that opens a menu, Excel will pop open that menu. If the second key miraculously happens to be one that starts a command, Excel obediently issues that command and might even open a dialog box. At some point you'll hit a key that Excel is not expecting. That's when it beeps at you.

3. **Why isn't my printer printing?**

Here's the situation. You print a worksheet. Five minutes later your printer is still quietly sitting there. There are no printed pages in sight. You try this a few more times, and it still doesn't work. What gives?

There are two possible explanations. If you're trying to print by clicking on the Print tool, make sure that you aren't really clicking on the Save tool. These tools sit side-by-side in the toolbar. If Excel displays a message saying that it *is* printing, but nothing comes out of your printer, your printer is off. Turn it on.

4. **My marquee won't go away**

Whenever you copy and paste in Excel, the marquee remains around the source cell. This is a gentle reminder to you that you can continue pasting copies of that same cell into other parts of the worksheet. Unfortunately, it makes most of us think that we did something wrong or left out a step. You know, "Hey Bob, the marquee's still there. What's up?"

Just press Esc to make the marquee go away. Better yet, when you move to the cell where you want to paste the copy, press Enter instead of choosing the Edit Paste command. This both pastes the copy and gets rid of the marquee.

5. **Where's the rest of my cell entry?**

When you type a really long entry into a cell, Excel usually lets it overflow into the next cell so that you can see all of it. But if the next cell already has something in it, Excel chops off the long entry at the right edge of its column. Use the Column Width command on the Format menu to increase that column's width so that you can see everything that's there.

6. **My text stays put when I use the Cut command**

When you choose Edit Cut to move the contents of a cell, Excel doesn't remove anything from the cell. To cut the information out, you first have to pick the destination cell and then choose the Edit Paste command. Until that time, Excel continues to show the marquee around the cell you're trying to cut.

7. **My Home key doesn't work properly**

Old habits are hard to break. Lots of other software programs let you press the Home key to move quickly to the top of a document. In Excel, pressing Home only moves you along the current row until it reaches the left edge of your worksheet. You have to press Ctrl+Home to get back to the very top of a worksheet.

8. **My column suddenly got very wide**
(Or, my row suddenly got very tall)

The dragging technique for highlighting a group of rows or columns is extremely close to the one you use for increasing column widths and row heights. The only difference between these two techniques is where your mouse pointer happens to be when you start dragging.

To select a group of rows or columns, be sure that your mouse pointer looks like a thick, white cross before you start dragging. To increase a column's width or a row's height, be sure that the mouse pointer is shaped like a thin, black cross before you start dragging.

9. **My formula answers look like text instead of numbers**

If you forget to start a formula with the equal symbol, Excel thinks you're entering text. Press F2 to edit the cell, hit the Home key to get to the left edge of the formula bar, type =, and then press Enter to store the entry. The cell now should show a number.

10. **When I select a cell range, Excel erases everything!**

You might experience this horror if you're a new mouse user. The action of selecting a range of cells involves clicking on the first cell, dragging to the last cell, and then releasing the mouse. When you click on the first cell, don't click on the small black handle in the lower right corner of that cell. That's the fill handle, and if you drag it, Excel will fill the entire selected range with whatever happens to be in the first cell. When the first cell is blank, Excel fills your entire selection with blank cells. The proper way to select a range of cells is to place the mouse pointer in the middle of the first cell and drag through the remaining cells.

11. **My worksheet just disappeared!**

Fortunately, worksheets don't really disappear unless you tell them to. You probably clicked on the Minimize button (▼) in the upper right corner of your worksheet window. Look at the bottom of your Excel screen. You'll see an icon with the name of your worksheet just below it. Double-click on the icon to get your worksheet back. (Or, if you haven't quite licked double-clicking yet, you can click on it once and press Enter.)

12. **All the information in my worksheet just disappeared!**

You either clicked inside one of the scroll bars or hit the PgDn key. Excel has scrolled out of the worksheet area that contains the information you typed. Press Ctrl+Home to get back to the top left corner of your worksheet.

12 Best Excel Shortcuts

1. Open Sesame

If you want to open a worksheet that you've recently worked on, open the File menu. The last four worksheets you opened are listed at the bottom of the menu. Click on the one you want.

2. Getting Excel under control

If you have lots of worksheets open, you can close them in one fell swoop. Hold down the Shift key, open the File menu (notice that the Close command becomes Close All), and choose the Close All command. Excel closes all worksheets.

3. Draggin' til you drop

Dragging and dropping in Excel is the quickest way to copy and move blocks of data around your worksheet.

To move a cell range quickly, highlight it, place your mouse pointer anywhere on the perimeter of the highlighted area, drag to where you want to move the data, and drop it there. The moved cell range appears instantly.

To copy a cell range quickly, highlight it, place your mouse pointer anywhere on the perimeter of the highlighted area, hold down the Ctrl key, drag to where you want to move the data, and drop it there. A copy of the cell range appears instantly.

4. 911 for emergencies, F1 for help

Whenever you're trapped, or lost, or in a bind, or confused, or unsure of how to proceed, or afraid to proceed, or unaware that you need to proceed, or just plain unaware, hit the F1 key. All your answers are there.

5. Closing Excel or a worksheet, lickety-split

At a recent Indianapolis 500 Speedway time trial, it was confirmed that the quickest way to exit Excel and get back to Program Manager is to press the keyboard shortcut Alt+F4. It gets you out in a flash.

During the same time trial, it was confirmed that the quickest way to close an Excel worksheet is to use the keyboard shortcut Ctrl+F4.

6. The shortcut menu shortcut

You can avoid Excel's Edit and Format menus altogether by using the shortcut menu. Just right-click your mouse in any cell or in a cell that's part of any selected cell range, and Excel will open its shortcut menu. From the shortcut menu, you can quickly cut, copy, paste, clear, delete, and insert data in your worksheets. You also can format numbers, align anything, change fonts, draw borders around cells, and add patterns.

7. The cell range selection two-step

Have you ever released your left mouse button too early while you were dragging through a cell range? If you have, then you know that you must start all over again in order to highlight all the right cells. Here's an easy way to include additional cells to a range that's already highlighted in your worksheet. It involves only two quick key presses.

Position your mouse pointer over the cell you want as the new bottom right corner of the highlighted block. Now hold down the Shift key and click your mouse once in that cell. Excel quickly adds all the in-between cells to the highlighted range.

8. **Best-fit column widths (and row heights, too)**

The best way to adjust column widths in a worksheet is to let Excel do it for you. Position your mouse pointer atop the vertical bar at the right side of a column's heading. When the pointer becomes a thin, black cross, double-click the left mouse button. Excel will expand or shrink the width of the column to match the longest entry in that column. To create a best-fit row height, double-click on the horizontal bar at the lower edge of a row's heading.

9. **Fast font flipping**

The Font list box in the Standard toolbar offers the fastest way to add new fonts to your worksheets. For some reason, when you have lots of different fonts installed on your computer, it can take from 5 to 10 seconds for the Font dialog box to appear when you choose the Format Font command. But it only takes about 1/10 second for the Font list box to drop down when you click on its down arrow.

10. **At the beep, the date and time will be...**

To quickly insert the current date, press Ctrl+; (semicolon).
To insert the current time, press Ctrl+: (colon).

11. **Quick formulas**

If you want to enter the same formula into several cells, select the range that will contain the formula. Type the formula in the first cell. Rather than press Enter to enter the formula, press Ctrl+Enter. The formula is entered into the active cell and all cells in the selected range.

12. **Sum speedy formula, huh?**

Oh, and last but certainly not least, the AutoSum tool. Where would we be without this one? Just move into the first blank cell

after the cells you want to sum, and click on the AutoSum tool. Excel immediately types a SUM function into the formula bar. It even supplies the range of cells you want to sum. Just press Enter for an instant answer to the function.

12 Features You Can Monkey with If You Have Time To Kill

1. Developing your own style

The longer you work with Excel, the more you'll develop your own style. Not the I-have-a-car-phone or let's-eat-sushi kind of style. I'm talking about the kind where you invent a method of making your worksheets look attractive. You can group together your favorite formats and give them a style name. Maybe you like using an Arial 16-point bold font with a single underline for your worksheet titles. You could call this the TITLE style.

To create a style, pick any cell in the worksheet and apply your favorite formats there. Now click inside the Style list (it's the box at the left end of the toolbar that always says *Normal*.) Type in a new name for your style. To apply this style to other stuff in your worksheet, move there and choose the new style from the Style list (click on its down arrow to open the list). If you're feeling real adventurous, you can edit your style list entries by using the Format Style command.

2. Summarizing worksheet data in an outline

Excel can create an outline for your worksheet data. With an outline, you can collapse rows and columns together so that only your report titles, headings, and totals appear on-screen. This makes it easy to print summary data instead of the entire worksheet.

Select everything in your data table. Open the Formula menu and choose the Outline command. Click on the Create button in the Outline dialog box. Excel shows its outlining tools in the left and top margin of your worksheet. To collapse all the rows in your table

and show only the column titles and the totals row, click on the minus button in the left margin. To redisplay the row detail, click on the plus button in the left margin. You can then use the minus and plus buttons in the top margin to collapse and then expand the column details. When you get the exact detail you need, print your report.

To get rid of the outline when you're finished, reset your data table so that all information shows. Then press Alt+Shift+Left arrow. Click on the Rows button in the Promote dialog box and click OK. Again, press Alt+Shift+Left arrow. Now click on the Columns button in the Promote dialog box and click OK.

3. **Goal-seeking for fun and profit**

The Goal Seek command solves formulas backwards. Imagine that the highest price you want to pay (tax included) for a car is $15,000. The sales price is in cell B1—but don't enter anything. You want Excel to figure out that value. In cell B2, enter a formula that calculates the sales tax:

=0.08*B1

In cell B3, enter a formula that calculates the total purchase price:

=SUM(B1:B2)

You want to figure out how much to offer for the car so that when the sales tax is added, the total price in cell B3 is $15,000.

Open the Formula menu and choose the Goal Seek command. Type **B3** in the Set Cell box; type **15000** in the To Value box; and type **B1** in the By Changing Cell box. When you're ready, click OK to solve this formula backwards. In the Goal Seek Status dialog box, click OK to return to your worksheet. In this example, when

the sales price is set to $13,888.89, the sales tax is equal to $1,111.11, so the total purchase price is equal to $15,000. You can press Ctrl+Z immediately to get your original numbers back.

4. **Pasting numbers that add up to something**

If you ever have two worksheet templates that contain numbers you want to add together, here's one way to do it all at once. (Be sure that the cell ranges you want to combine are the exact same size before you try this.)

Open both worksheets in Excel. Select the range of cells in the first worksheet. Choose the Copy command from the Edit menu. Press Ctrl+F6 to show the second worksheet. Activate the first cell of the same range in the second worksheet. Open the Edit menu and choose the Paste Special command. In the Paste Special dialog box, click on the Add button and then click OK. Excel adds the numbers from the first cell range to those in the second cell range. For even more daring calculation escapades, try using the Subtract, Multiply, and Divide options in the Paste Special dialog box.

5. **Counting beans with the Analysis Tools feature**

For those of you who are dying to perform complex statistical analyses with your worksheet numbers, boy do I have the thing for you. Open the Options menu and choose the Analysis Tools command. Excel presents you with a list of the 19 most-loved statistical calculations of all time. From multi-variable regressions to two-factor anovas without replication, the Analysis Tools feature has it all. (Let's hope you know what you're doing, because I have no idea how these tools work.)

6. **Using Excel's canned macros**

Excel comes with a whole slew of prefab macros called "add-ins" that can do different things for you. For example, there's an

autosave macro that automatically saves your worksheets for you, and there's a macro that lets you add notations and summary information to your worksheets. When you start one of these add-ins, Excel adds a description for the macro to one of the menus. The AutoSave macro, for instance, gets added to the Options menu. To see what's available on your computer, choose the Options Add-ins command. You can use any of the macros that appear in the dialog box that opens.

7. Making workbooks

In Excel, a *workbook* is a collection of worksheets, macros, and charts. You create a workbook because it allows you to group together the documents that belong together. It's like having a briefcase in which you can stick all of your important folders. When you want to work with a particular group of documents, all you need to do is open the workbook file, and Excel instantly opens every document that's part of that workbook. Workbooks are a time-saver.

To create a workbook, open all the worksheets, macros, and charts you want to include. Then open the File menu and choose the Save Workbook command. Give your workbook a descriptive name like FINANCE.XLW, BUDGETS.XLW, or CASHFLOW.XLW. Later, when you open the workbook, Excel opens all the related documents you saved within it.

8. Controlling how Excel calculates

Doesn't it seem like there would be only one way to calculate formulas in your worksheets? Well, Excel gives you not one, not two, but *three* different ways to calculate formulas. Open the Options menu, choose the Calculation command, and take a look. You can have Excel calculate for you automatically, you can make Excel wait until you press F9, or you can let Excel calculate some things

automatically and others not. As if that's not enough, there are no less than eleven other options for fine-tuning your calculations. And you thought adding was as easy as 1-2-3.

9. **Blending colors in the color palette**

When you choose the Color Palette command on the Options menu, Excel shows you the Color Palette dialog box—a palette of the sixteen colors available to you in various parts of the Excel program. For special color needs, you can edit a color in the palette by using Excel's Color Picker tool (hey, I don't make up these names, I just report them). To edit a color in the palette, click on the color and then click on the Edit button. Excel displays the Color Picker dialog box. Feel free to picker any color you think will do the job. To picker a color, clicker it once with your mouser. Then clicker OK once to return to the Color Palette dialog box. Your new color appears in place of the one you edited. You can use the new color in cell patterns, text color, or anywhere in a chart that uses color.

10. **Toolbar face-lifts**

Not only can you display other toolbars in Excel and then arrange them all around your workspace for the ultimate in convenience, but you can even add a custom picture to the face of any one of the tools. Before you try this out, you need a picture; create something in the Paintbrush program. When you finish making the picture, save it. Now copy the picture to the Clipboard. (Most Windows-based graphics programs let you press Ctrl+Ins to do this.) Now switch to Excel. Open the Options menu and choose Toolbars. Then click on the Customize button in the Toolbars dialog box. Click on the tool you want to customize, open the Edit menu, and choose the Paste Tool Face command. Voilà! A toolbar face-lift in under 10 seconds flat.

11. The macro, just another object

Macros are simple enough to start when you've given them short-cut names like Ctrl+Z or Ctrl+G. After you create ten or twenty macros, it can get a little bit confusing trying to remember which shortcut key runs what macro. If it will help you keep track of your macros, you can attach them to objects in your worksheets. Anytime you click on the object, a macro runs. Maybe you'd like to run a formatting macro as soon as you click on an embedded chart. To attach the macro to the chart, be sure that the appropriate macro sheet is open in Excel; then right-click on the embedded object to display its shortcut menu. Choose the Assign Macro To Object command. In the Assign To Object dialog box, click on the name of your macro and click OK. Whenever you move your mouse pointer over an object that's attached to a macro, you can click on that object to run the macro.

12. Taking copious notes

It would seem that creating a report and typing it into a worksheet would be all you need to do to document important data. But in this age of telecommunications and high-speed data transfer, we all seem to want to know more about everything. So maybe the Excel worksheet's no exception. If you want, after you type a number into a cell, you can attach a lengthy diatribe to the cell so that the 24th-century explorers who one day unearth the worksheet will know exactly what it's all about. To add notes to cells, open the Formula menu and choose the Note command. In the Cell Note dialog box, type your earth-shattering news into the Text Note box. Be sure that the address in the Cell box belongs to the cell you want to annotate. Click on Add to add the note, then OK to get back to the worksheet. If you really want to make this a multimedia miracle, click on the Import button and choose a .WAV sound file to add to the note. That way, whenever someone reads the cell's note, your worksheet will break into the 20th-century rendition of Beethoven's Fifth Symphony.

I HATE

Index

Symbols

A

B

G-H

X-Y-Z